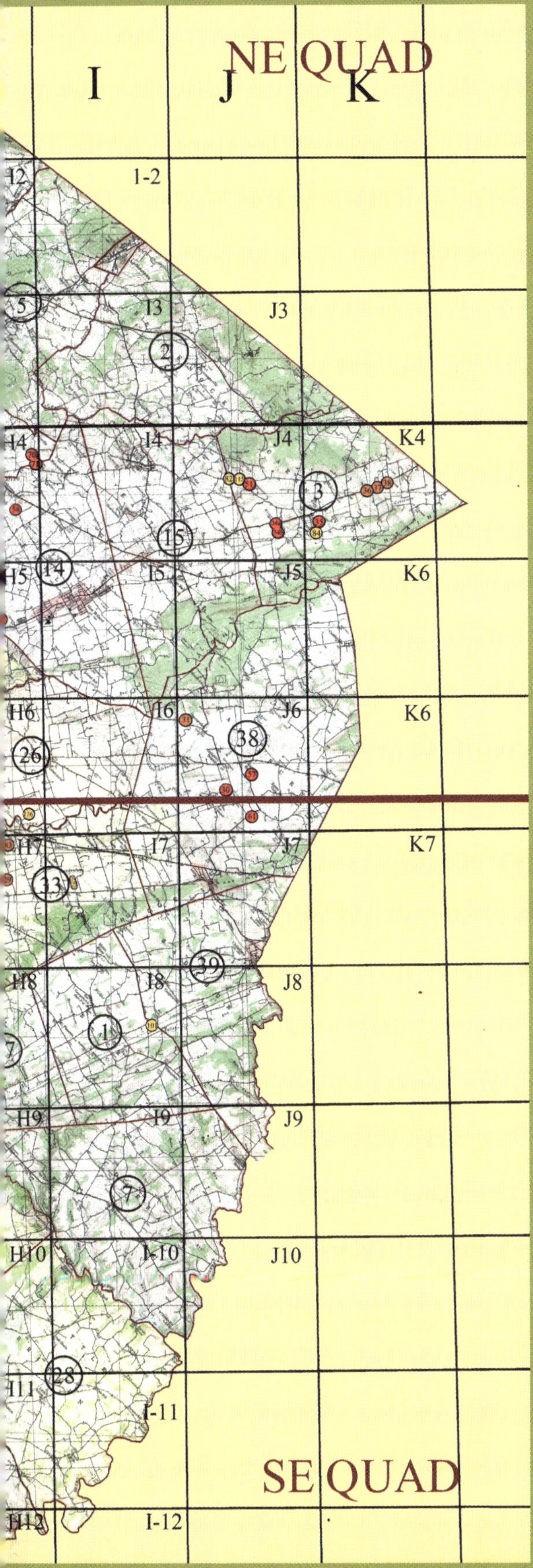
NE QUAD
I
J
K
I-2
I3
J3
I4
J4
K4
I5
J5
K6
I6
J6
K6
I7
J7
K7
I8
J8
I9
J9
I-10
J10
I-11
SE QUAD
I-12

The Story of Lime
and the

Lime Kilns

of Lancaster County

Kenneth G. Miller

SCHIFFER PUBLISHING®
4880 Lower Valley Road • Atglen, PA 19310

A Pennsylvania Dutch family, ca. 1900, removing burnt lime from their large three-burner lime kiln in this copy of the large-format "3-D Art" work of Aaron Zook. *Photographed by the author with permission of the owner, Abner Zook, son of the deceased artist*

Library of Congress Control Number: 2020930936

Edited by Ian Robertson
Designed by Jack Chappell
Cover design by Jack Chappell
Type set in Baskerville/Minion

ISBN: 978-0-7643-6073-2
Printed in India

Published by Schiffer Publishing, Ltd.
4880 Lower Valley Road
Atglen, PA 19310
Phone: (610) 593-1777; Fax: (610) 593-2002
E-mail: Info@schifferbooks.com
Web: www.schifferbooks.com

To my father, Martin K. Miller, and mother, Mabel (Gerlach) Miller, who passed on to me a Godly heritage, and whose lives and love I dearly miss.

And

To Dr. Alex Henderson II, mentor, colleague, and dear friend, and to whom, more than anyone else, I owe my career in the Biology Department at Millersville University.

Contents

Foreword

Lancaster County Pennsylvania enjoyed the reputation of being a "Green Garden" as early as the mid-eighteenth century and the "Garden Spot of America" by 1800. That brand—derived from the county's lush and productive farm culture—endures today. One of the secrets of the Garden Spot's wide repute lay in its limestone soils and limestone rock. Chunks of limestone rock—burned to an intense heat of 1500 degrees Fahrenheit—produce an ash lime powder, similar in color and consistency to flour. Lime played three important roles in Lancaster's agrarian economy. First, farmers spread the white dust on their fields to "sweeten" the soil by lowering its acidity (pH), often caused by the high acidity of cattle manure. Blending the "sweet" lime and the "sour" cattle manure produced the bumper crops that contributed to Lancaster's robust Garden Spot standing. Second, lime served as a "glue" in the mortar that held stone and brick foundations and walls intact for barns, homes, and other buildings. Lime was also necessary to make plaster to seal the inside walls of buildings. Finally, lime was used as a disinfectant or sanitizer in rural homes and barns well into the twentieth century.

Still, how could the typical 19th-century farmer acquire lime? A farmer constructed a homemade lime oven or kiln to produce lime for himself and other farmers in the neighborhood. The *1875 Atlas of Lancaster County* identifies 525 small private lime kilns in Lancaster County at the peak of homemade lime production. All of these lime kilns have fallen into ruin and disappeared. Large commercial kilns expanded in the twentieth century, leaving the small kilns in the dust bin of history.

In this marvelous book, Professor Miller captures in photo, graphics, and text the story of 126 small Lancaster County private kilns in various stages of decline. None of these existed in 1875, and many of them will surely vanish by the end of the twenty-first century. Professor Miller's exquisite photography and his careful scientific description will forever preserve this important cultural key that helps to explain Lancaster's stellar agricultural reputation that emerged in the eighteenth and nineteenth centuries. Miller situates Lancaster's lime kiln story within the larger international history of lime that reaches back to the Neolithic period with a kiln in Israel that dates to 10,800 BCE.

We owe enormous debt and great gratitude to Professor Miller for his diligent and persistent research over more than a decade that has culminated in this significant and fascinating book.

Donald B. Kraybill, PhD, is a distinguished college professor and Senior Fellow emeritus at the Young Center for Anabaptist and Pietist Studies at Elizabethtown College. He has published more than a dozen scholarly books on North America's Anabaptist groups, including *The Riddle of Amish Culture* and *Horse and Buggy Mennonites: Hoofbeats of Humility in a Postmodern World*, both of which focus on Lancaster County. Kraybill served as the acquisitions editor for the Anabaptist and Pietist series published by Johns Hopkins University Press.

Preface

The Lime Kiln Project

This book had its beginnings after I retired from a career of teaching. Two years at Solanco High School, in southern Lancaster County, were followed by thirty-three years of teaching and research in ecology and natural history at Millersville University.

Upon my retirement in 1993, my first project was an attempt to photograph all the butterflies native to Lancaster County. This took me to all corners of the county, focusing on the butterfly "hotspots." After I had recorded some ninety species, it was becoming more and more difficult to find the rare ones. It was time to turn to another project.

By now I was into my second Panasonic Lumix digital camera, and I decided to focus my lenses upon the old nineteenth-century stone lime kilns found along the back roads throughout this "garden spot" of agriculture.

I soon came to realize that while all lime kilns are basically alike, each one has its own unique features. Fascination and curiosity drew me on, and I rediscovered the old adage that "the more I learned the less I seemed to know!" I wanted answers to so many questions. How old was the kiln? When was it built, and by whom? How were these kilns used? How did they work? There had to be more of them out there. How could I find them? What about the greater story of lime burning? When did it first begin, and where? Surely there was a body of literature to be found. The project exploded.

Friends and many Amish farmers whom I talked to asked some of the same questions I had. I began to devote more and more time to literary research and to traveling the county in search of more lime kilns, getting tips here and there, with the goal of finding all the extant kilns in the county, just as I did the butterflies. Early on I realized that, at least for now, I would have to limit my work to Lancaster County.

This project was fast becoming more than a collection of photographs, and it gradually became obvious that it was growing into a book, although two stories were emerging. There is the story of the lime kilns of Lancaster County, and then there is the larger story of lime itself. I have tried to weave these into a single book.

I trust that you will enjoy reading this work as much as I did putting it together.

—Kenneth G. Miller

Acknowledgments

How do you acknowledge so many people who have had some part in the creation of this work? Chris Stoltzfus would be the first. As a young man Chris worked in his father's lime kiln—one that was built by his grandfather, near the eastern Lancaster County village of Churchtown, who is the local authority on the subject. In our conversations he provided me with valuable information and shared a copy of his "scrapbook" on lime, a copy of which is on file in the library at Poole Forge.

Amos Hoover is the founder and curator of a valuable library on Anabaptist history, and an excellent farm museum, housed at the Fairmont Retirement Community on the top of the hill near Farmersville. He offered personal information and translated a valuable document with reference to lime burning from Pennsylvania German to English.

Ivan Glick (deceased), a local historian and writer, shared a number of conversations, and especially his experience and photographs while helping to burn a lime kiln that Amos Long restored near Herndon, Pennsylvania.

I am grateful for the generous help of the staff members at various museums and libraries throughout the county, including the Mennonite Historical Society, the Lancaster Historical Society, the Lancaster County Archives, and the Cocalico Historical Society.

I cannot begin to list the many conversations I had with farmers—frequently Amish—and their permission to take pictures of old lime kilns on their farms, and the untold number of people and friends who offered leads, tips, and directions to little known kilns.

I appreciate the encouragement and editing given by my daughter, Donna Osborne.

A sincere thank you to Dr. Donald Kraybill for kindly writing the foreword.

I am grateful to the loving support and encouragement of my dear wife, Dottie, who put up with my frequent forays off scouring the countryside, or hiding away in my study while neglecting chores around the house and garden, and who helped with the preparation and editing of the manuscript.

And a special thank you to the editorial staff at Schiffer Publishing for their kind assistance and guidance through the publishing process.

May I also add that I wish to thank the Lord my God for leading me into this project and allowing me to see it to fruition. As a wise man once said:

"Trust in the Lord with all thine heart, and lean not to thine own understanding. In all thy ways acknowledge him and he shall direct thy paths" Proverbs 3:5-6

Prelude

The Eureka Moment

We can only imagine how lime was discovered. Most certainly it was as a white crust that formed on some of the rocks around hearths and campfires. Possibly the children laughed with glee as it bubbled and fizzed when a bit of water was accidently spilled. In the shadows we see an older, bright young mind watching . . . watching and wondering, especially when later discovering that some of these stones were cemented together. Here was one who wondered about many things, but now it was about the white crust. Fascinated, he realized that with this white crust he could intentionally make two objects adhere to one another.

In that moment, lime was discovered!

God gave us insight into "cause and effect" in the world around us. But only so often does a mind come along that is capable of grasping this concept better than others. Here was one of these minds, and this was one of those "eureka" moments, a moment of discovery, a moment that would change the world.

Perhaps it was a young man who took advantage of his new discovery to affix a small, shiny stone to a little piece of wood, along with a "string" woven from the vine of a climbing fern, and presented it to a special lady friend. The practice quickly spread when she proudly adorned herself with this talisman by displaying it around her neck.

This is an imaginary story, of course, and no matter how it may have occurred, this seemingly small step signaled a gigantic leap in the emergence of modern civilization. That this paste could be used intentionally to cement objects together seems to be such an obvious conclusion that one would expect it to have been a common practice among aboriginal peoples. Perhaps it was.

A handful of lime

ONE

Lime: Its Ancient Origin and Evolution

A Brief Overview of Lime

Lime (calcium oxide)—or *quicklime*—is a white, alkaline, caustic, powdery material that is manufactured by heating limestone and other calcareous materials such as coral or mollusk shells in a "lime oven" or *lime kiln* to a temperature of approximately 900°C (± 1600°F).

Lime is one of the world's most widely used natural resources. We say *natural*, even though it is actually a modified substance that is produced directly by "burning" or roasting limestone in "lime ovens" or lime kilns. It was used by ancient people more than 16,000 years ago, as supported by archeological evidence from the Sinai Desert, where small stone artifacts were found bearing traces of lime paste used to cement them onto handles or shafts of arrows and spears (Kingery et al. 1988). Eventually, other uses were discovered for this amazing material, and in time it became common practice to spread lime-based plasters and mortars over floors and walls, and to line graves, bins, and cisterns, where precious water could be stored in the desert. It was also found to be a wonderful material out of which to sculpt effigies, and to decorate ceremonial skulls and other objects (Rollefson 1983).

Archeological evidence suggests that it is undoubtedly the oldest *manufactured* substance—one where human intervention produces something new, something that did not exist before. Today the world manufactures more than 350 million metric tons of lime annually, nearly two-thirds of it by China (International Lime Association 2017).

Architectural uses of lime originated as early as ca. 10,000 BCE (Haklay and Gopher 2015), with the practice spreading throughout the Middle East and Mediterranean, eventually reaching its zenith among the ancient Greeks and Romans, who turned it into a highly developed technology. Their architecture and its endurance are marveled at today by engineers who are constrained to reinforce their concrete with steel. The Romans constructed the architectural wonder known as the Pantheon of lime-based concrete, still standing in all its glory, without reinforcing materials.

The dome of the Pantheon, completed in Rome by Hadrian in 123 CE. Its lime-based concrete dome is 142 feet in diameter, the same as its height. Built entirely without reinforcement, it is 23 feet thick at its base and 2 feet thick at the oculus on top. *Courtesy of the photographer, Brandon Voight, who owns all copyrights to its use*

Roman farmers may have had some knowledge of the horticultural benefits of lime, though it was not until sixteenth-century Britain that it came into use as an important soil builder, sweetening the ground and greatly increasing the land's productivity. In 1675, John Worlidge, quoting from the *English Improver*, wrote the following:

> Liming of the Land is of moft excellent ufe, many barren parts of this Nation being thereby reduced into fo fertile a condition for bearing moft forts of Grain, that upon Land not worth above two or three Shillings an Acre well husbanded with Lime hath been raifed as good Wheat, Barley, white and gray peafs as England yields (Worlidge 1675).

Liming, as it is known, is widely practiced today throughout the modern world, although much of it is done by spreading pulverized, unburnt limestone, now known as *ag lime*.

As the ancient use of lime spread through the Middle Eastern Levant and beyond, its production developed into a community endeavor, with the stone being burned in open pits. In time these pits were lined with stone and partially enclosed to conserve heat and manage the draft. The rise of the Roman civilization led to an increased demand for lime, along with the development of more-efficient ovens: kilns that could be kept burning continuously, feeding in stone and fuel, and producing lime in an ongoing process.

With the decline and fall of the Roman Empire, advanced technology in lime burning and the manufacture of concrete was essentially lost. Along with many other developments, it had to be more or less reinvented during the Renaissance, when these skills were needed to build huge forts, castles, and cathedrals throughout the Western world (Johnson 2009). Fortunately, some technologies were preserved during those "Dark Ages," notably within the abbey walls of the church.

A Maya temple complex in Palenque, Mexico. Temples were built of stone and were heavily coated with a lime-based plaster. *A digital painting by the author after Harenburg*

At approximately the same time that the use of lime was spreading throughout the Mediterranean and Europe, huge amounts were also being produced by Mesoamerican cultures, most notably the Maya, a description of which is summarized succinctly (Negrón et al. 2015), as follows:

> Powdered lime was one of the most important materials produced and utilized by the ancient Maya. It was a key ingredient in the mortar used to construct monumental edifices and residential structures, as well as in the lime plaster that coated the facades, floors, and interior walls of these structures. Lime was even crucial for maintaining a viable maize-based diet through the *nixtamalization* process.

This widespread use of lime in two opposite hemispheres would suggest that its discovery occurred multiple times in various places around the world.

The Discovery of Lime

Our story unfolds in the northern Sinai Desert, along the banks of the Wadi Lagama. In the far-distant past, a hunting party passed this way during the favorable times of the year, when the wadi ran cool and clear. Birds and other small game were plentiful among the reeds.

Several of the men worked at knapping small fragments of flint, while others prepared an adhesive of lime paste to haft the flint spear-points and arrowpoints onto shafts. We can only speculate on the source of the calcium they used. It may have come from the white crust formed on the rocks of the hearth. Possibly they heated the little white nodules of limestone that had been found at the site, or they may have heated snail shells, gathered from the marsh, until they turned white from calcination. Small amounts of travertine—a form of limestone precipitated naturally from some springs and small ponds in the mountains—may have

Chipping flints in the Sinai approximately 16,000 years ago. *Digital painting by the author*

Location of the Lagama North VIII archeology site in the northern Sinai desert. N30.805844 E33.459452.

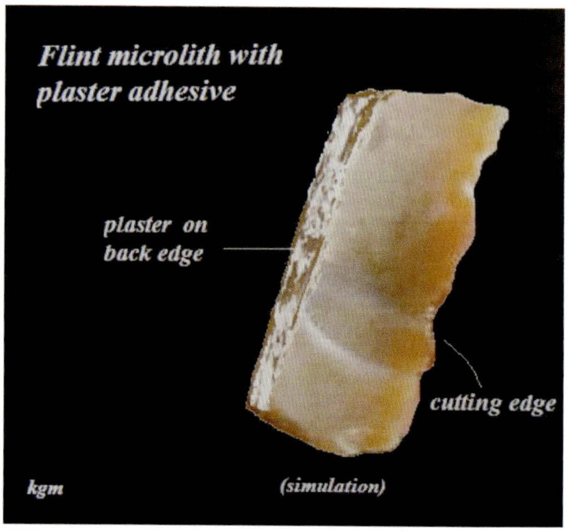

An illustration showing how lime paste was applied to the edge of a flint microlith

Examples of microliths attached to shafts of spears and arrows

been collected and burned in the hearth. Bones of land animals, fish, and birds are also an excellent source of calcium. Whatever source was found, by the twentieth century, archeologists would determine it to be pure lime paste (Kingery et al. 1988).

It was many thousands of years later when another party came across the remains of that ancient campsite and discovered many of these tiny chips scattered and buried in the sand. This was a party of archeologists, and they immediately recognized these chips as *microliths* (miniature stones); some of them still bore evidence of the lime paste. It appears that more than 16,000 years ago, the people at this site now known as Lagama North VIII were making and working with lime. It is the earliest evidence of lime ever found.

A Google Earth map of the eastern Mediterranean, showing the location of Hayonim Cave between the Dead Sea and the coast. N32.920089 E35.211863.

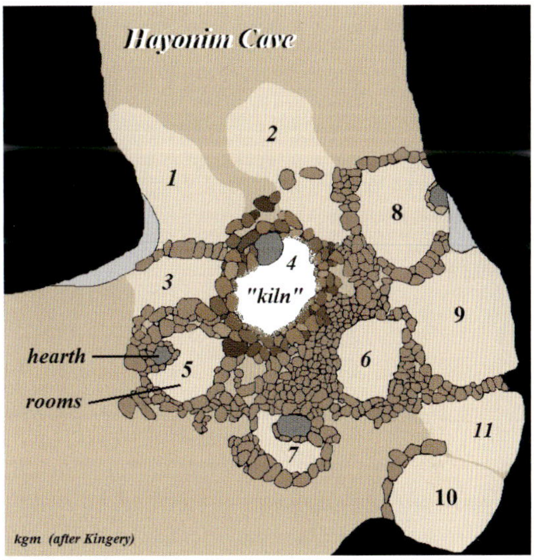

A diagram showing the location of structures, including the "lime kiln," inside Hayonim Cave. *Digital drawing by the author, after Belfer-Cohen*

Hayonim Cave in the Galilean Hills of northern Israel. *Courtesy of Dr. Carol Stiner*

The First Known Lime Kiln

In the course of time, other uses were discovered for this amazing material that we now know as lime paste, which after applied would harden like rock. In fact, it became common practice during the Neolithic period (ca. 10,000 BCE in the Near East) to spread these lime-based plasters and mortars over walls and floors and to line graves, bins, and cisterns (Clarke 2012).

Very little evidence of the actual preparation of lime has been found. The limestone was fired in pits and various impermanent chambers that quickly disappeared. One notable example is a "room" within Hayonim Cave, in northern Israel. Archeologists, excavating layers of deposits dated to approximately 10,800 BCE, discovered that one of the "rooms" in the cave was used to burn lime (Kingery et al. 1988).

No doubt other "lime kilns" will be discovered as archeologists continue to explore the hidden world beneath our feet. Evidence of a lime kiln nearly 2,000 years later (10,400 calibrated years before present [cal BP], roughly 8000 BCE) has also been reported more recently (Toffolo et al. 2017) at the Nasher-Ramla quarry in Israel, and a lime kiln in Mesopotamia from 2450 BCE is frequently referenced in literature and often reported to be the oldest lime kiln ever found.

The Beginnings of Architectural Lime

On this semiarid hillside (*pictured*) about 16 miles north of the Sea of Galilee, overlooking Eynan Spring and the fish ponds of the fertile Hula Valley, we find remains of the ancient village of Ain Mallaha.

Evidence suggests it was occupied over a period of approximately 3,000 years (15,000 to 12,000 cal BP) by people of the Natufian culture. Excavation of this site has revealed many clues about life and conditions at that time. It bears evidence of the beginnings of agriculture and is considered to be among the earliest permanent human settlements (Haklay and Gopher 2015).

Here, more than fifty circular and semicircular, one-room "huts" have been uncovered, some paved with stone slabs and partially enclosed by stone walls. Lime plaster was found in the excavations, although it had not yet come into common use. One house from the Early Natufian phase (14,326 cal BP) was coated with a red-painted lime plaster (Valla et al. 2017), and Shelter 1 has no perimeter wall but a lime plastered bench (5 meters in diameter) in layer II, the last of the early Natufian occupations (approximate radiocarbon age of 14,326 ± 266 cal BP; Haklay and Gopher 2015).

The archeological site of the Neolithic village of Ain Mallaha (Eynan), overlooking the northern end of the Jordan valley. *Google Earth image, 2018*

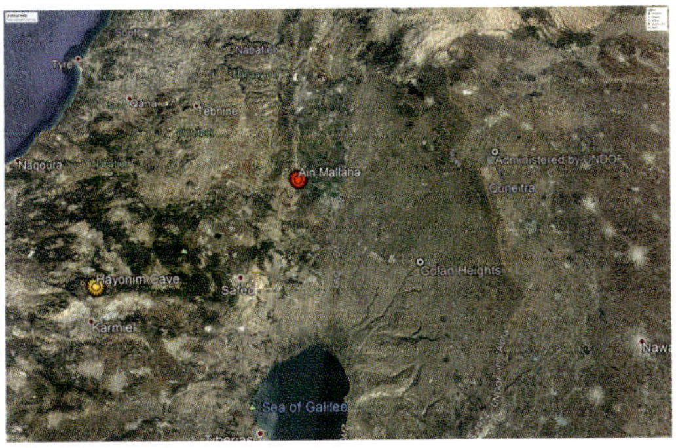

A Google Earth map showing the location of Ain Mallaha approximately 13 miles north of the Sea of Galilee. N33.080612 E35.573014.

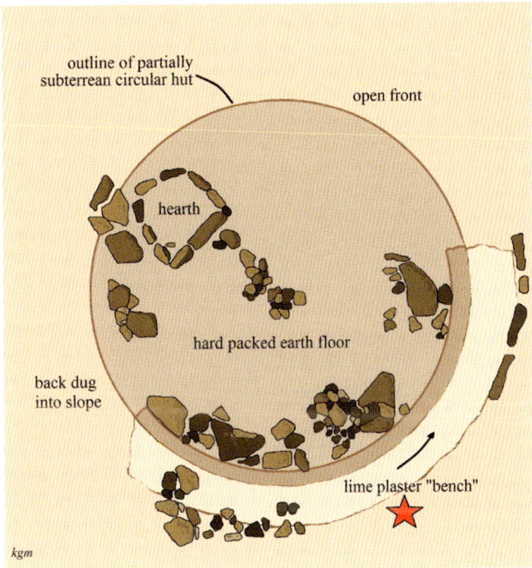

A schematic diagram showing the excavated interior of Shelter No. 1 and the location of the plastered bench. *Drawing by the author after Haklay and Gopher 2015*

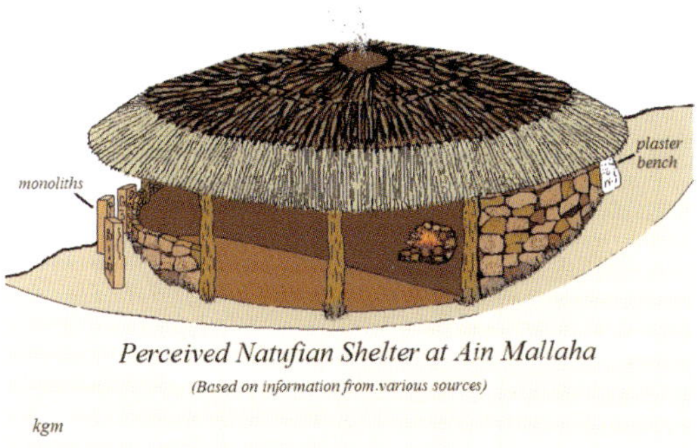

An artistic rendering of Shelter No. 1. The plastered bench is on the right rear of the structure. *Digital painting by the author after Haklay and Gopher 2015*

Lime in Ceremonial Structures

Gobekl Tepe

On the Konya Plain, in southeastern Turkey, 35 miles north of the Syrian border, a prominent feature known locally as Gobekli tepe (the potbellied hill) rises out of the barren limestone plateau. Flat, rectangular rocks poking to the surface of the hill have for generations vexed local farmers and in 1996 aroused the curiosity of German archeologist Klaus Schmidt (Schmidt 2010). Little did anyone imagine that these stones would turn out to be the tops of huge monoliths, each reaching down to their base 20 feet below the surface of the hill.

Beginning around 11,000 years ago, with nothing more than stone tools, a hunter-gatherer people began to create what turned out to be one of the most astonishing ritualistic complexes of Neolithic times. Schmidt, until his untimely death in 1961, had been leading the excavation of this incredible complex of circular and oval enclosures, each ranging from 10 to 30 meters in diameter. These structures were enclosed with stone walls, incorporating in the ring as many as twelve huge, T-shaped monoliths weighing up to 10 tons and more. Two similar but larger pillars were set into sockets carved into the limestone bedrock in the interior of these enclosures. These gigantic monoliths were carved from a single blank in a quarry 300 meters away. Many were covered with elaborate carvings of animals and designs (*see illustration*). The pillars were found in layer III, dated to the 10th millennium cal BP (Schmidt 2010), between 9600 and 8000 BCE.

Floors of some of the enclosures were made of terrazzo—limestone chips embedded in a highly polished plaster matrix believed to be made with burnt lime (Schmidt 2009). Similar floors were found by Schmidt at Nevali

The archeological site of Gobekli tepe, dated as early as 9000 BCE. *Digital painting by the author after Teomancimit 2011*

A Google Earth map showing the location of Gobekli tepe, north of Syria, in southern Turkey. N37.223047 E38.922348.

One of the more elaborately carved monoliths in the Gobekli tepe ruins. *Digital drawing by the author after Steinhilber*

Çori, a previously excavated site in the area carbon-dated to 8620 BCE, and at Jericho (7000 BCE; Kenyon 1957.

Even though, sadly, Schmidt died in 2014, the work goes on. Ground-penetrating radar has indicated that sixteen or more of these enclosures still lie beneath the surface of the mound. It seems that at some point in their "use," each of the enclosures was deliberately and completely filled in, so that by 8000 BCE the entire complex was out of sight, buried beneath the surface of the hill (Schmidt 2012).

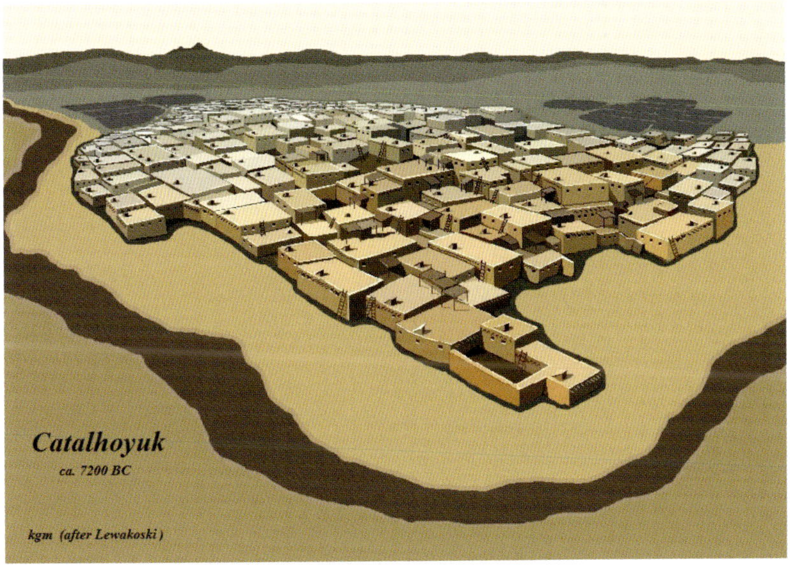

Çatalhöyük, Turkey, envisioned roughly 7000 BCE. *Digital painting by the author after a painting in Lewandowski 2014*

Çatalhöyük

In the Konya basin of south-central Turkey, approximately 25 miles southeast of the city of Konya, two large mounds rise conspicuously 20 meters above the surrounding plain. Once separated by a channel of the Carsamba River, the larger eastern mound encases one of the largest villages of the Neolithic period. The site was discovered in 1958 and excavated through 1965 by English archeologist James Mellaart, after which work fell idle for the next twenty-eight years (Mellaart 1967).

The site was revisited in 1993 by Ian Hodder of Stanford University, who continues today as the project director (Hodder 2006).

The artistic rendition (*above*) shows a large, compact community resembling a huge, sprawling motel of many apartments that housed at its peak a population of 10,000 people. The settlement was begun 9,400 years ago, at a time when the only tools were those made of stone and when farming was in its infancy. The excavators calculated the earliest occupation in the lower levels at 7500 BCE and the top layers at 5600 BCE, with the peak around 7000 BCE.

All the houses fit tightly together like a huge 3-D jigsaw puzzle of blocks, with little if any space between them, in a complex not unlike the adobe dwellings of the southwestern United States. These houses lacked passageways or streets, and the only entry was through hatches in the roof. While some stone was used in the walls, most were made of sun-dried mud bricks that are lavishly coated with plaster. Some rooms had as many as 450 layers.

Most of the plaster was made of locally abundant limey mud. At the lowest level of Mellaart's excavation (about 7500 BCE), Hodder and his team found chunks of burnt lime, and the use of burnt lime on floors that were covered and painted with polished lime plaster. The archeologists suspect that the use of lime during the earlier stage of the settlement was given up because it required too much fuel, and adequate plaster could be readily made from locally abundant limey "mud" (Hodder 2006).

The site is known for its early, lavish use of artwork. The interiors of some buildings are remarkably adorned with enclosed hearths, clay bowls, astonishing wall paintings, and hangings. Sculpted heads of the auroch, many with real horns, are ubiquitous. Some of their dead were buried beneath the floors—a common practice throughout the Neolithic Near East. No evidence of communal buildings have been found, and it is puzzling how the social and religious structure of the community was maintained.

A Google Earth map showing the location of Çatalhöyük, in south-central Turkey. N37.666377 E32.827245.

An excavated room in the Çatalhöyük complex. *Digital drawing by the author after Drgulcu 2008*

Ain Ghazal

While excavating the Amman-Zarqa highway on the outskirts of Amman, Jordan, in the 1970s, a bulldozer operator cut into some old ruins. The site, which was subsequently systematically excavated by archeology teams led by Dr. Gary Rollefson from 1982 to 1989, revealed one of the oldest and largest cities of ancient times. Houses were built on terraces above the Zarqa River while the inhabitants farmed the surrounding hillsides. Seasonally, a large population left the city, taking their herds with them to graze the plateaus to the east (Rollefson 1983).

Here we find an explosion in the widespread use of burnt lime. It was a time when people began to expand the architectural use of lime throughout the Levant, and here was a classic example. They built their houses of stone and mud bricks, and then, after heavily plastering them with mud inside and out, they finished with a layer of lime. Floors of cobble were coated with lime and painted with a highly polished red pigment. Lime paste was used to make small figurines of human and animal shapes. Thousands of these images were discovered during the excavations; whether they were religious objects or toys remains unknown.

Many burials were discovered beneath the floors of occupied houses. Skulls were frequently separated from the bodies; many were coated with lime paste and decorated realistically. The most remarkable discovery was several cashes of hobbit-sized plaster human torsos. They were shaped with lime plaster that was worked around a core of reeds and painted with lifelike facial features. Several lime-burning pits (lime kilns) were found on the site.

Ain Ghazal began as a small village nearly 10,000 years ago along the banks of

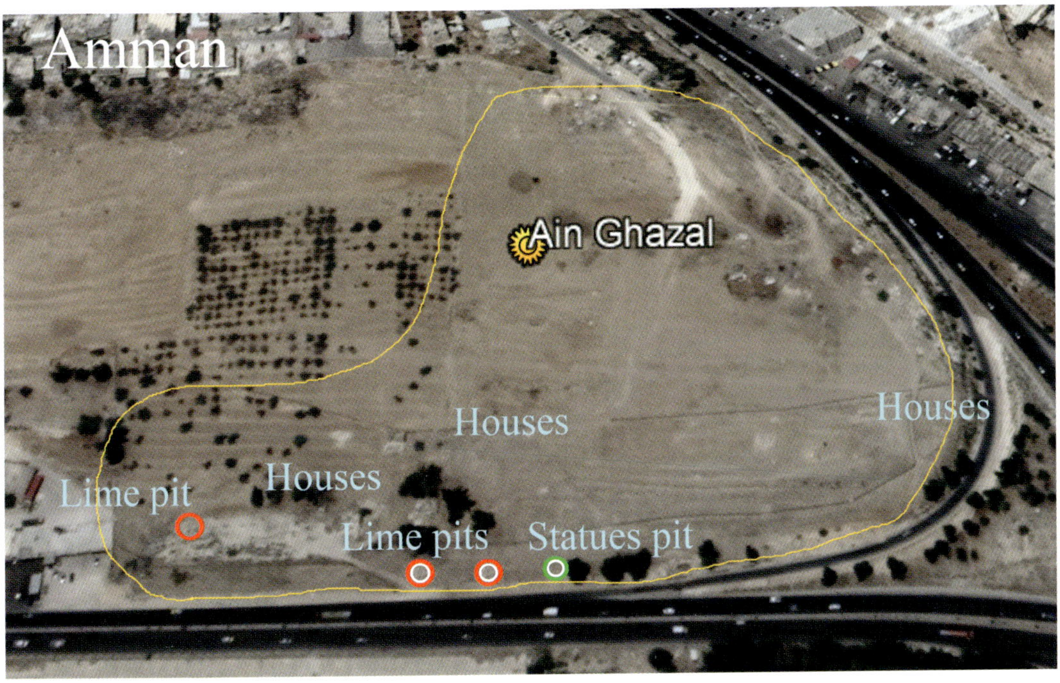

Ain Ghazal Archaeological Area; a labeled Google Earth aerial view of the site

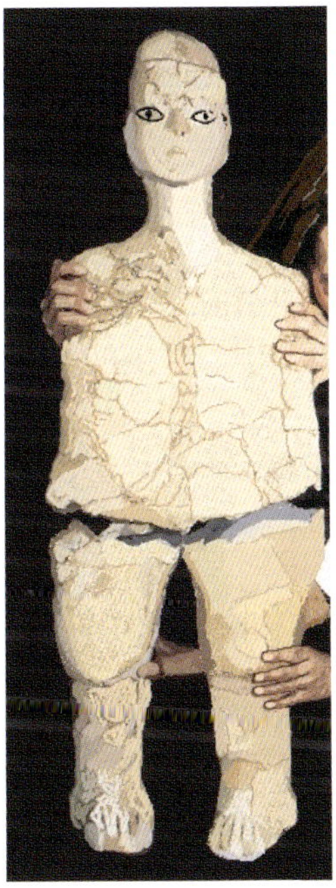

A view of one of the reconstructed "hobbit-sized" human statues uncovered in a pit during excavation of the Çatalhöyük ruins. *Digitally drawn after a photo in an article (Rollefson 1998)*

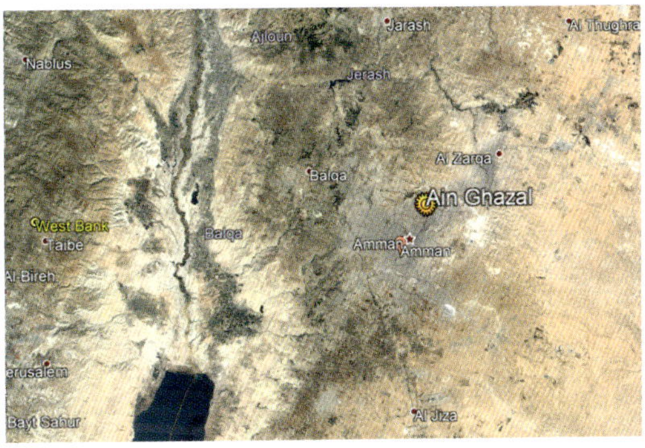

A Google Earth map showing the location of Ain Ghazal, approximately 30 miles north of the Red Sea, in Amman, Jordan. N31.986556 E35.976057.

the Zarqa River. It was a time when people, previously living in nomadic bands, began settling in sedentary groups, experimenting with agriculture and domestication. The settlement grew rapidly and prospered for an astonishing 2,000 years, reaching its zenith around 7000 BCE with a city of more than 3,000 people.

Around 6500 BCE the city began a rapid decline and had within half a century dwindled to a handful of houses. It seems likely that the concentrated population outgrew its subsistence level.

It would be another several thousand years before we again see lime used as extensively as it was during this Neolithic period in the Levant of the Middle East.

A lime-plastered floor of an excavated building in Ain Ghazal. *Digital painting by the author, after Rollefson 2013*

Crete

Lime Moves West

The complete story of how lime made its way from the Middle East to Europe is yet to be constructed, but it is probably safe to say that it was an integral part of the western movement of civilization from the Levant and Anatolia throughout the Aegean, Crete, Greece, northern Italy (Etrusca), and Rome in a very convoluted and indistinct way.

When changes are found in a particular culture, it is rarely clear where the impetus came from: whether they were "invented" from within, were brought home by travelers, or were introduced by visitors, or the indigenous population was displaced by immigrants. With the decline of the Neolithic cities and towns of the Middle East, the use of architectural lime declined substantially. As civilization spread, it appears that lime plaster continued to be used here and there, principally in floor coatings and wall plaster. This was especially true in the important buildings of the cities.

Knossos, Crete

It was during the Minoan civilization, which developed on the island of Crete during the years from approximately 3000 to 1100 BCE, that lime plaster was again widely used to coat the floors and insides of buildings such as vaults and burial chambers. Walls of buildings were made of mud, brick, and stone coated with lime plaster.

The center of the Minoan civilization was the palace at Knossos south of Heraklion, 3 miles inland from the coast. It was first excavated in 1878 by Minos Kalokerinos of Heraklion, followed by Sir Arthur Evans, Oxford scholar and professor, who purchased the tract in 1895 and oversaw the excavations for the next thirty years, exposing the remains of a Neolithic civilization and the magnificent Palace of Knossos (Evans 1921–1936.

Evans believed that the site was first occupied in Neolithic times, around 8000 BCE. The Minoans are known for their extensive development of the art and technology, including the production of large fresco murals made by applying pigments to a wet coating of lime plaster. Magnificent scenes such as the "bull leaping" (*above*) from the Palace of Knossos covered large portions of walls of public buildings, palaces, and villas of the wealthy on Crete and throughout the Aegean and Mediterranean, from Egypt to eastern Anatolia, Greece, and Italy. Writing in Warren 1972, M. A. S. Cameron argues that

> Crete's greatest achievement in the field lay in a certain technical mastery of the materials, notably in the use of lime plaster such as rarely employed elsewhere at the time. Only, it seems at Catal Huyuk some three or four thousand years earlier (7500 to 5600 BC) were somewhat similar lime plasters manufactured (Cameron 1972).

The famous "bull-jumping fresco" restored from the Temple of Knossos, on the island of Crete, dates to the Final Palace period, ca. 1450–1400 BCE. *Digitally repainted by the author after an image in an article by McInerney in* Expedition

An aerial view of the partially restored Palace of Knossos on Crete. N35.299745 E25.159266. *Downloaded from Google Earth*

Egypt

The literature on the Egyptian use of plaster, though plentiful, is confusing and inconsistent. Earlier accounts claim that the great pyramids were coated with lime, and contend that they had lime through all the periods of their history, as far back as 3000 BCE or more.

As early as 1865, William Wallace analyzed samples of plaster from the Great Pyramid and reported that "it consists of 81.5 percent calcium sulfate and only 9.5 percent of the carbonate" (Wallace 1865).

In 1904, Auguste Choisy claimed that the "Egyptians employed a mortar made from burnt gypsum and never used lime" (Choisy 1904). Finally, Alfred Lucas, in his quintessential work of 1934 and reprinted as recently as 2012, titled *Ancient Egyptian Materials and Industries*, argues that "there is little evidence that the Egyptians knew of lime before the Ptolemic Period" (305 to 30 BCE). Lucas and coauthor J. R. Harris claim that the controversy arises from the fact that the calcium carbonate reported in many samples of mortar and plaster from ancient tombs and palaces occurs incidentally, originating from the sand and other materials used in making the mortar (Lucas 1962; Lucas and Harris 2012).

The fact that modern analysis finds most plasters have a complex and varied composition, with calcium carbonate ranging from trace amounts to 40 percent or more, would suggest that in some instances at least, the Egyptians did use limestone in significant amounts.

Even though limestone is plentiful in the Nile valley, it requires a sustained heat of 1500–1600°F for calcination, whereas gypsum begins to calcine at temperatures as low as 200°F, with 400 degrees being commonly used. That is roughly one-third the heat for making lime. With the fuel required to burn large quantities of lime being limited in the Egyptian desert, it is understandable that they would favor gypsum in their plasters and mortars.

It may be of interest here to note another controversy or curiosity a bit out of the mainstream regarding the casing stones that once completely enshrouded the pyramids. They are generally accepted as being highly polished white limestone obtained from quarries across

The Pyramids of Giza, ca. 2500 BCE. *Digitally painted and modified after Liberato 2006*

the river at Tura. All but a handful of these huge stones have been removed and used in other projects around Egypt. A small number still cap the peak of Khafre's Pyramid, in the middle of the complex, and a short section that was discovered under rubble at the base of the Great Pyramid (*above*).

In 1940, French materials scientist Joseph Davidovits set the geological and Egyptology communities on their heels by claiming that the ancient blocks of the giant pyramids were made of "concrete" cast on-site. He has engineered a material he calls *geopolymer* that he claims is similar to those stones. Although the idea is largely rejected, in 1980 Michael Barsoma of Drexel University examined specimens of the pyramid stones and concluded that at least some of the stones of the pyramid were indeed castings (Jana 2007).

A short section of the external casing uncovered at the base of the Great Pyramid. *Digital painting by author after Bodsworth 2007*

TWO

The Lime Kiln
(Panorama of Shertzer's Meadow Lime Kiln)

The Lime Kiln

Introduction
An Old Tale from Nathaniel Hawthorne

Bartram, the lime-burner, a rough, heavy-looking man, begrimed with charcoal, sat watching his kiln, at nightfall, while his little son played at building houses with the scattered fragments of marble, when, on the hill-side below them, they heard a roar of laughter, not mirthful, but slow, and even solemn, like a wind shaking the boughs of the forest . . .

Bartram and his little son, while they were talking thus, sat watching the same lime-kiln that had been the scene of Ethan Brand's solitary and meditative life, before he began his search for the Unpardonable Sin. Many years, as we have seen, had now elapsed, since that portentous night when the IDEA was first developed. The kiln, however, on the mountain-side, stood unimpaired, and was in nothing changed since he had thrown his dark thoughts into the intense glow of its furnace, and melted them, as it were, into the one thought that took possession of his life. It was a rude, round, tower-like structure, about twenty feet high, heavily built of rough stones, and with a hillock of earth heaped about the larger part of its circumference; so that the blocks and fragments of marble might be drawn by cart-loads, and thrown in at the top. There was an opening at the bottom of the tower, like an oven-mouth, but large enough to admit a man in a stooping posture, and provided with a massive iron door. With the smoke and jets of flame issuing from the chinks and crevices of this door . . .

There are many such lime-kilns in that tract of country, for the purpose of burning the white marble which composes a large part of the substance of the hills. Some of them, built years ago, and long deserted, with weeds growing in the vacant round of the interior, which is open to the sky, and grass and wild-flowers rooting themselves into the chinks of the stones, look already like relics of antiquity, and may yet be overspread with the lichens of centuries to come.

"Tending the Kiln." *A photo of Deafy's Den Lime Kiln "photoshopped" by the author to represent a scene from* Ethan Brand, *a short nineteenth-century novel by Nathaniel Hawthorne*

Evolution of the Lime Kiln

For thousands of years, lime was burned in open pits (*right*), as seen from these ancient remains in the Jordanian desert. This type of kiln was used throughout the ancient world on into modern times, including the American frontier. It is no doubt used today at places when a small amount of lime is needed.

To construct such a kiln, a shallow hole is dug—preferably into a bank or hillside—and is often lined with stones. The bottom is filled with fuel such as sticks and branches, and then chunks of limestone are thrown in on top. More fuel would be added as the stone was filled in. Typically the whole mass would be covered with soil or sod and fired. After a period of time—several days or more—the remains would be shoveled out and the burnt lime separated from the ash and poorly burnt stone. Improvements in this design include a more permanent, neatly worked stone enclosure and a tunnel-like entrance at the bottom where more fuel may be added as the burnt lime is removed.

It is not known when the first modern-style lime kiln was invented—that is to say, one that we would recognize as a lime kiln of today. Likely it was a Roman development. Possibly it was in Neolithic Mesopotamia.

While excavating the Oval Temple site at Khafajha (possibly as early as 2500 BCE), Delgougaz identified a number of ovens in various houses. One oven associated with the temple

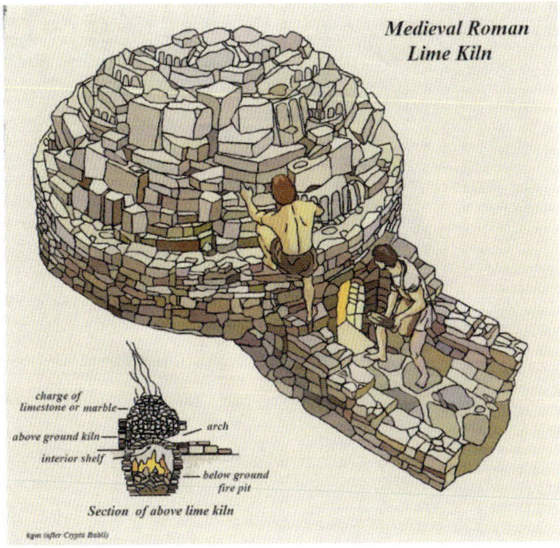

An "improved" pit kiln. *Digital painting by the author of Crypta Balbi, after Manacorda 2002*

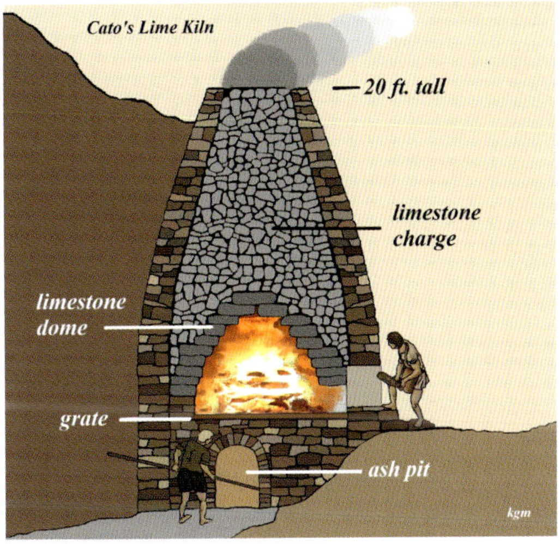

Cato's Kiln. *Digitally painted by the author after a description in "De Agricultura, by Cato the Elder," Cato the Elder 1934*

An ancient lime pit at Grayn fort, near Ras al Naquab, southern Jordan. N30.095645 E35.470244. *Photo taken by Dan Gibson, 2001, and used here with permission*

ruins yielded a grayish-white substance not found in other ovens, which, upon chemical analysis at the Berlin State Museums, proved to be chiefly calcium carbonate. Delgougaz concluded that this structure was at some time used to burn lime. If correct, this would be the earliest true lime kiln structure yet discovered. The temple has been assigned to the Early Dynastic III period (2650–2350 BCE; Delgougaz 1940).

An improvement over the simple pit kiln was the addition of chambers, above and below, such as we see here in this early medieval lime kiln inside the Cryptabalbi in Rome (Gering 2014; based on a sketch in Arce 2003 credited to Sagui L. 1993).

We know that in the second century BCE, Cato—the Roman soldier, statesman, and farmer—in his *De agricultura* described the design of a farm lime kiln that was virtually identical to our eighteenth- and nineteenth-century kilns. In Cato's design, a "dome" of larger, flatter stones was carefully laid up on the base, serving as the fire chamber that supported the smaller stones filled in from above. As the fire burned, the dome of stones would be consumed into lime, until the entire charge eventually burned into a mass of lime and collapsed. If an iron grate was used, the ashes would fall through and be separated from the lime (Cato the Elder 1934).

Domed Charge vs. Layered Charge

There were two basic ways to load a batch kiln, referred to here as (1) the domed charge and (2) the layered charge. In the former, the archway opens directly into the pot, as shown in the "open arch" photo. When the kiln is loaded, a dome-like structure of larger and flatter stones, such as Cato describes, is carefully built up on the floor of the kiln. This structure then serves as the primary fire chamber. The charge of smaller limestones is then filled in on top of this dome. A set of iron bars may be placed temporarily across the arch opening to hold in the stones. As the heat from the wood fire burns into and up through the dome, more fuel may be added from below until the entire mass eventually collapses to the floor of the kiln. The bars are then removed and the burnt lime and ash is drawn out through the arch. The only apparent difference between most post-Renaissance kilns and Cato's kiln was his narrow opening at the top of the pot.

With the layered method (2) and the accompanying "closed arch" photo, the rear of the archway is permanently walled up, with a small opening—the draw hole—at the bottom. The fuel may be added and burnt lime withdrawn through this smaller opening. Iron bars are placed across the kiln, several feet above the floor, to support the limestone charge. The burnt lime is either drawn out through the draw hole or shoveled out from the top.

An archway partially closed off at the back, with a large doorway opening into the pot. *Myers Kiln South*

An archway opening directly into the pot of the kiln. *Poole Forge Kiln*

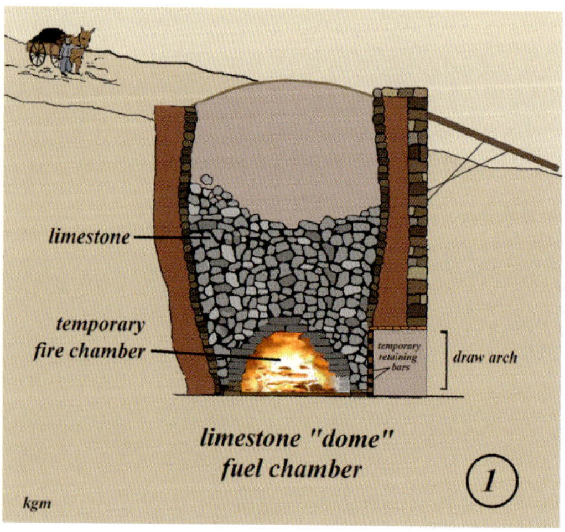

A fuel chamber dome constructed with large, flat limestones. *Freehand digital drawing by the author*

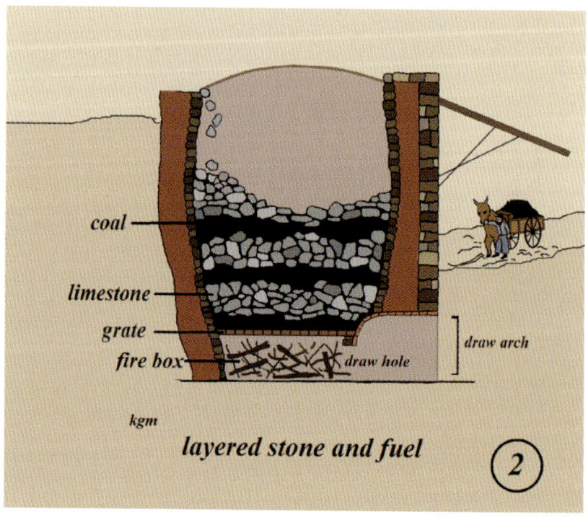

A lime kiln charge with layered limestone and coal. *Freehand digital drawing by the author*

Batch Kiln vs. Perpetual Kiln

Through the years, lime kilns underwent many iterations to improve their efficiency, such as Erb's Lime Kilns (*below*) from a 1907 calendar. In the very center of the photo is a dark, rectangular stone structure. This is a batch kiln, likely Mr. Erb's first kiln, probably built in 1886, when he went into the lime business. It would have represented the typical rural farm kilns during the eighteenth and nineteenth centuries. When burning in these kilns, a layer of fuel (wood in earlier times and coal later) was spread on top of a pile of kindling, followed by a layer of limestone, then coal and stone layered in to the top, where it was covered with a layer of coal dust and soil that would slacken the fire and allow the temperature to be regulated by the kiln tender poking holes through the top. When the stone was calcined after several days to a week, the batch was allowed to cool and the lime was removed through the arch at the bottom. Then the process could be repeated.

The following tale was told to me by members of the Erb family:

An archway closed off at the back, with a small, square draw hole. *Peoples's Hatchery Kiln*

Erb's Lime Kilns, showing a perpetual kiln (white shed and tall stack) and a batch kiln (boxlike stonework behind and left of the white shed). *Courtesy of the Erb family*

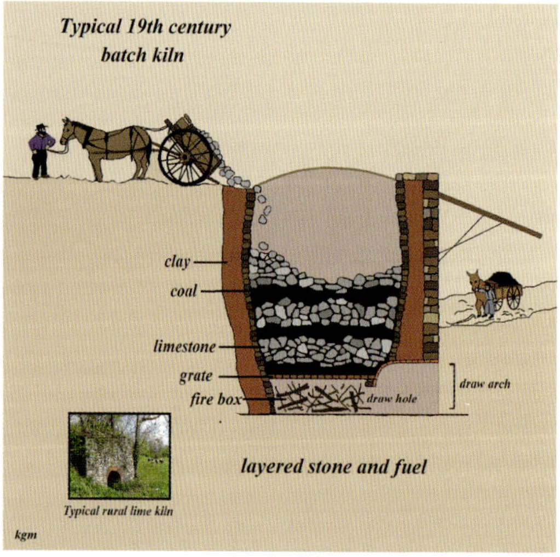

Section of a batch kiln with a layered charge. *Freehand digital drawing by the author*

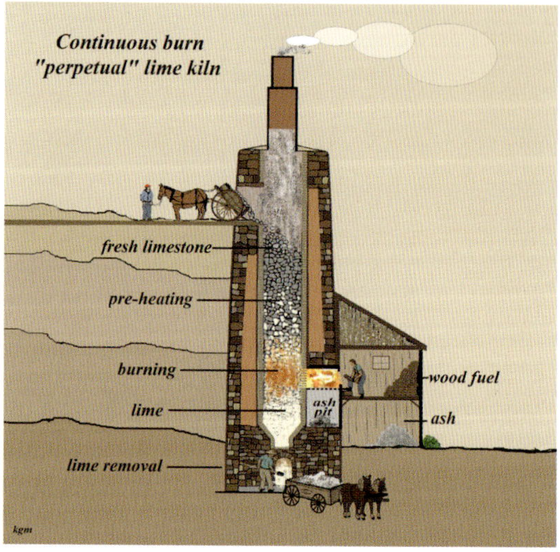

Section of a perpetual kiln, showing the offset fire chamber. *Freehand digital drawing by the author*

Grandpa Erb [Thomas H. Erb Sr.] it seems was quite a character. When he came "of age" his father bestowed upon him a sum of money which he could use either to attend college or start a business. Well, he chose college and enrolled at Millersville State Normal School. We're not sure just how long that lasted, but one night he and some of his cohorts rounded up a goat and ran it down through the women's dormitory, a prank that got them all expelled. That was the end of college for Thomas Erb Sr., but the beginning of a successful business career. On November 11, 1886, for $65, he purchased the rights to build a lime kiln and start up a lime and stone business.

The business prospered, and at some time prior to 1907 he added the perpetual kiln, the tall structure in back of the white shed in the calendar image. In these new kilns, sometimes referred to as patent kilns, stone was added from the top, and fuel created the heat that was directed into the kiln partway down. This was an ongoing process, allowing the burnt lime to be continually removed from the bottom until the kiln was shut down for repairs,

Aboriginal Papua New Guinea native burning coral to produce a small amount of lime. *Digital painting modified from several sources by the author*

Copy of a woodcut from an old Chinese book, showing a man burning a pyre of limestone and coal. *Digital painting by the author after* Chinese Technology in the Seventeenth Century *by Sung Ying-Hsing, reprinted in 1996*

A crew of workers posing at their recently built lime stack (rick) near Mount Joy, Pennsylvania. *From an old photograph courtesy of Mrs. Joanne Heller*

A circular oyster rick built of cordwood, such as is burned from time to time at Williamsburg. *Digital painting by the author*

A colonial-period crib-style kiln used to burn oystershells. *Digital painting by the author*

A typical Maya lime stack using a chamber of vertical green logs. *Digital painting by the author as depicted in a scene in the movie* Apacolypto, *directed by Mel Gibson*

A lime stack such as might be used in rural Mexico. *Digital painting by the author*

or possibly some other reason. These perpetual kilns were used commercially until more-advanced, gas-fired tall stacks and horizontal rotating kilns were developed.

Miscellaneous Open Burning

Through the years and around the world, localized variations appeared in the way lime was burned. In some places these methods are still used today.

Modern Horizontal Rotary Kiln

This brings us to the highly complex mechanized process widely used today: the horizontal rotary kiln. The design was first patented by Thomas Russell Crampton in 1877, and later by Frederick Ransome's patent of 1885, followed by further improvements by various companies in the United States, until it was perfected to the point where the rotary kiln has evolved into the premier design for the commercial lime-burning industry (Lahovsky 1980; Gan 1997; Moore 2017).

The rotary kiln consists of a long, cylindrical steel tube typically several hundred feet long, 8 to 10 feet in diameter, and lined with firebrick. This huge tunnel slopes gently downward, rotating slowly at about 2 rpm, which gradually tumbles the limestone downhill, moving through hot gases and flame. It is calcined along the way and exits at the lower end after 1.5 to 2 hours. All the while, fresh limestone is added at the upper end so that it is a continuous operation. This is a rather simple explanation, since many complex modifications are often employed for specific kilns (Boateng 2008).

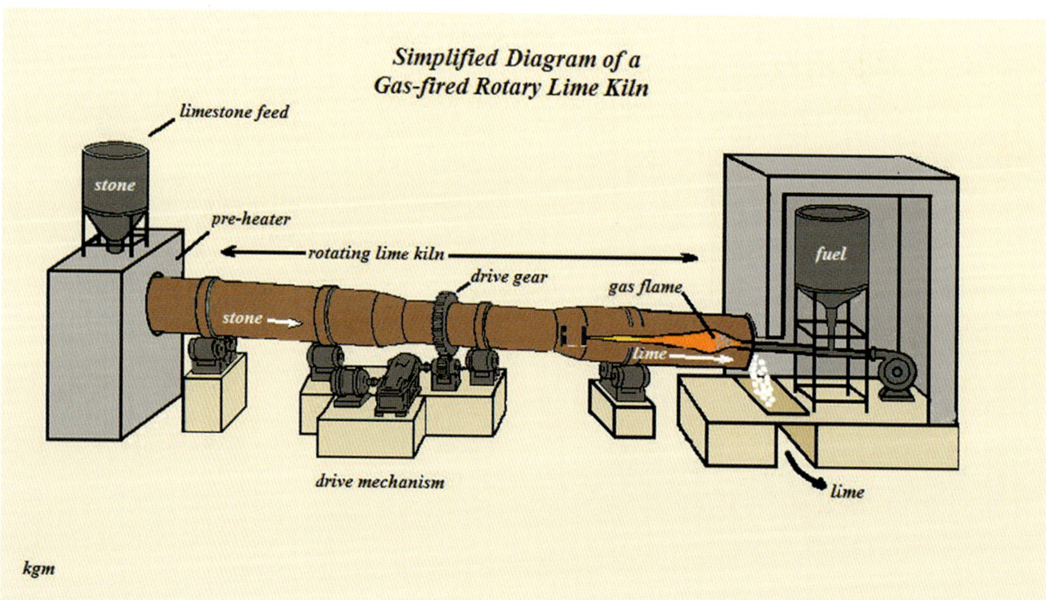

A simplified diagram of a horizontal gas-fired rotary lime kiln. *Digital painting by the author*

Aerial view of a double rotary kiln at Magnesite Refractories (York, Pennsylvania) Lime Plant. *Downloaded from Google Earth*

THREE

Making lime in the meadow. *Photo by author from 3D Art by Aaron Zook*

The Lime-Burning Process

A cutaway model of the lime kilns at Poole Forge, showing the empty pot on the left, while the one on the right is filled with a layered charge. *Model and photo by the author*

How It Works

Burning lime was hard and dangerous work, and many a limeburner was injured or lost his life in the trade. The process begins in the stone quarry, where the rock is blasted out and then broken down with sledgehammers into "the size of a man's head," then hauled by wagon to the kiln.

The pot is then loaded by spreading alternating layers of stone and coal, and heaped up at the top with small stones, coal, and dirt, into which draft holes may be punched. In the early days, wood was used as fuel, but most burners switched to coal as it became more available and less expensive late in the nineteenth century.

As the fuel burns, the limestone is converted into quicklime that accumulates at the bottom, where it is raked out through the draw hole or the main arch (or both) to be spread on fields or used to make mortar, plaster, or whitewash.

Today, quicklime is produced in huge industrial complexes—much of it in China—for hundreds of different uses, much of it in the construction and steel industry. Although some burnt lime may still be used in agriculture, the principal soil amendment today is ag lime (crushed unburned limestone).

Arthur Long, a modern-day limeburner, with chunks of limestone ready for burning in his kiln. Arthur restored his kiln near Herndon, Pennsylvania, and burned it for demonstrations for several years until his death. *Photo courtesy of Ivan Glick*

An old photo of the Wambold family men at work in their quarry near Limeville, in eastern Lancaster County, ca. 1900. *Courtesy of the Wambold family*

The Process Continued

Filling "Longie's" kiln with modern-day "horsepower" during one of the demonstration burns. *Photo courtesy of Ivan Glick*

Looking down into the white-hot burning limestone at a demonstration burn on Bob Shirk's farm near Churchtown, Pennsylvania. *Courtesy of Amos Stultzfus*

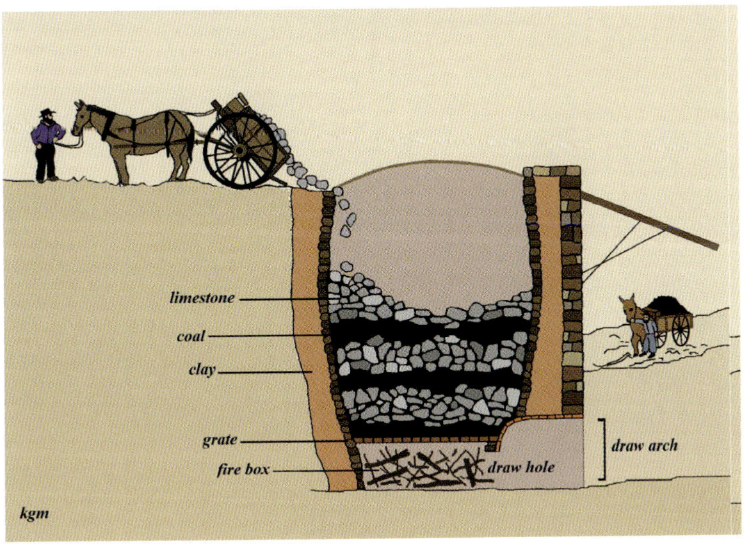

In earlier days the limestone was hauled from the quarry to the kilns in small wagons, using old-fashioned "horse power." *Digital painting by the author*

"Longie" cleaning out the burnt lime (quicklime) at one of his demonstration burns. *Photo courtesy of Ivan Glick*

"Longie's" grandson, George, scoops a handful of powdered lime from a barrel in the lime shed near the kiln. *Author*

Fire in the kiln on "demonstration day." *Photo courtesy of Ivan Glick*

The Lime Cycle

Limestone consists primarily of the mineral calcium carbonate with varying amounts of impurities, depending on the deposit.

When the temperature inside a burning kiln reaches 1500°F, a chemical change takes place. The calcium carbonate, $CaCO_3$, releases carbon dioxide, CO_2, and the limestone is transformed into quicklime calcium oxide, CaO. This process is known as calcination.

Quicklime is very unstable and reacts violently with water, H_2O, converting it into a new product, calcium hydroxide, $Ca(OH)_2$, slaked lime, slack lime, or hydrated lime. Quicklime may be applied directly to fields, where it undergoes "air slaking" and is worked into the soil in the spring, sweetening the soil and increasing crop production. Alternately, lime may be slaked directly in a large container or pit and used to make mortar, plaster, or whitewash.

After the mortar, plaster, or whitewash is applied, it begins to take up carbon dioxide from the air, converting it back into calcium carbonate again. Although the crystalline structure may not be the same, the result is chemically nearly identical to the original limestone, thus completing the "lime cycle."

The Lime Cycle. *Photo and layout by author*

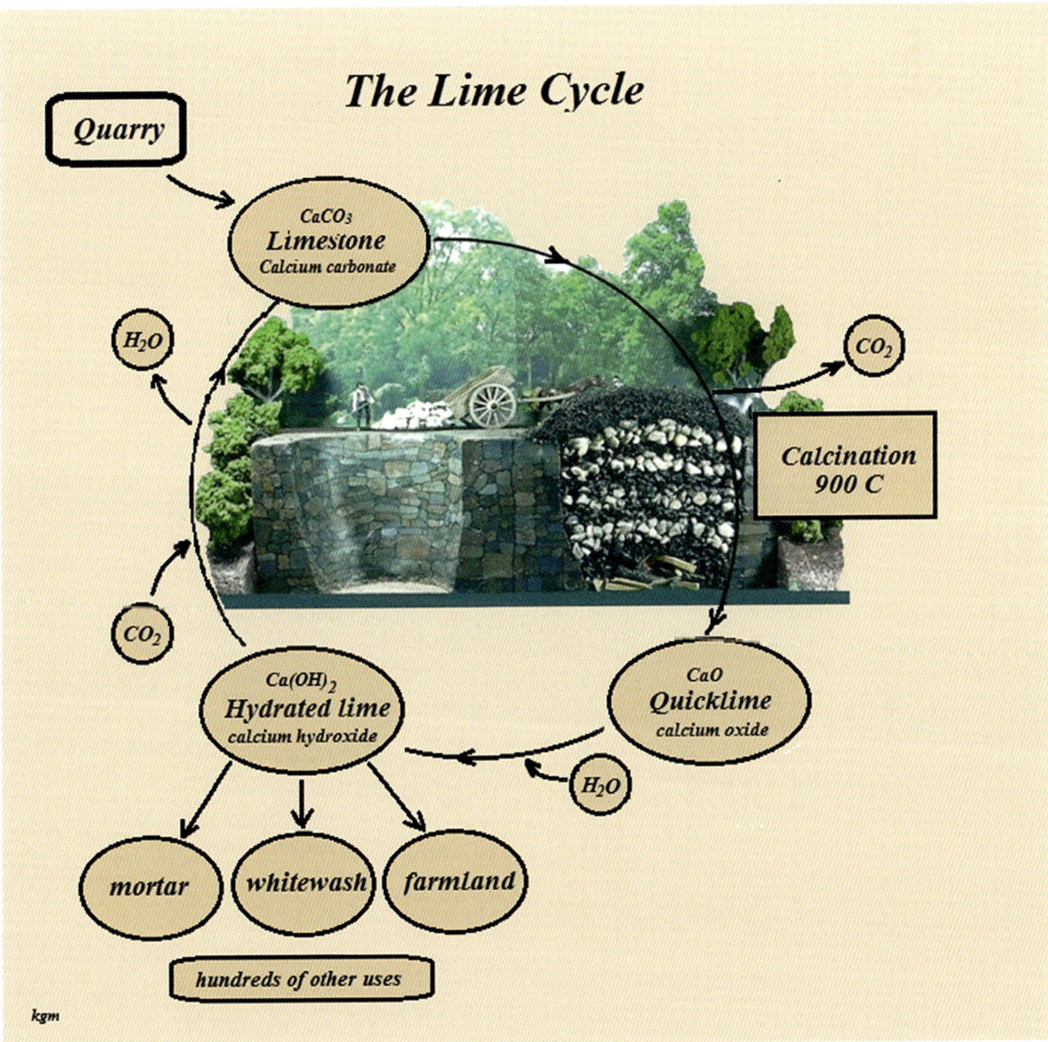

Farmer spreading lime. *Digital painting by author*

Rural Uses of Lime

Today there are hundreds of applications of quicklime in agriculture, manufacturing, and the chemical industries, with the production of steel and construction ranking among the major uses.

In earlier days back on the farm, many had their own kiln to burn enough lime for themselves and possibly a few neighbors. It was important to have enough lime to sweeten their fields to compensate for the vast amount of cattle manure that was applied. The secret to successful farming, they said, was "lime and manure." They learned that cattle and crops went together if you wanted to be a good farmer.

Pennsylvania Germans were among the first to learn—or we might say relearn—this "secret," since it was practiced among English and Welsh farmers as early as the fourteenth century or even before, as noted:

Year 1342: In *The Agrarian History of England and Wales*, we find that "There is one good instance in Shropshire of lime being used for improving marginal land being brought into cultivation . . . part of the same operation in 1342. . . . Presumably this lime dressing complemented the marling" (Hallam and Thirsk 1988).

Year 1594: Sir Hugh Plat (1653, first published in 1594), writing in his *The Jewel House of Nature*, says: "In the grounds bordering upon the woods of Arden, which are very cold, they ufe lime inftead of dung, and thereby they make the earth moft fruitful that was barren before."

Year 1602: In John Norden's *Survey of Oswestry, 1602* (reprinted in Slack 1951), regarding the limestone quarries on Brynogarth Mountain: "The lyme stones are of good use in the country to make lyme for the land." See also *The Itinerary of John Leland* (Smith 1907), which contains John Norden's *Survey of Oswestry, 1602*, on p. 61 (LO89).

Year 1618: John Norden, in *The Surveyor's Dialogue (1618): A Critical Edition*, writes, "Farmers do buy, dig, and fetch limestones, 2, 3, 4 miles off, and in their fields build lime kilns, burn it and cast it on their fields, to their great advantage" (Netzloff 2016).

Regarding the early medieval use of lime in Britain, we find an interesting quote from an early-thirteenth-century book, writing about King of Wales, Gruffydd ap Cynan, as follows: "He also made Gwyedd to glitter then with lime-washed churches, like the firmament with stars" (Jones 1910).

Early Lancaster County farmers were known for their stone barns and houses, which required large amounts of lime to make the mortar for building with stone or brick, to plaster inside walls and often the outside of their buildings, and for making whitewash, which was applied over stable walls, fences, the inside walls of houses, and a myriad other things as a preservative and to just "make things look nice." They also considered it an important sanitizer for many things around the barn, and there was always the ubiquitous bucket or barrel of lime in the outhouse for a scoop to be added down the hole before you left.

Laying a stone wall with lime mortar. *Digital painting by author*

Whitewashing the garden fence. *Author*

Plastering a wall with lime-based plaster. *Digital painting by author*

Lime barrel in the outhouse. *Digital painting by author*

FOUR

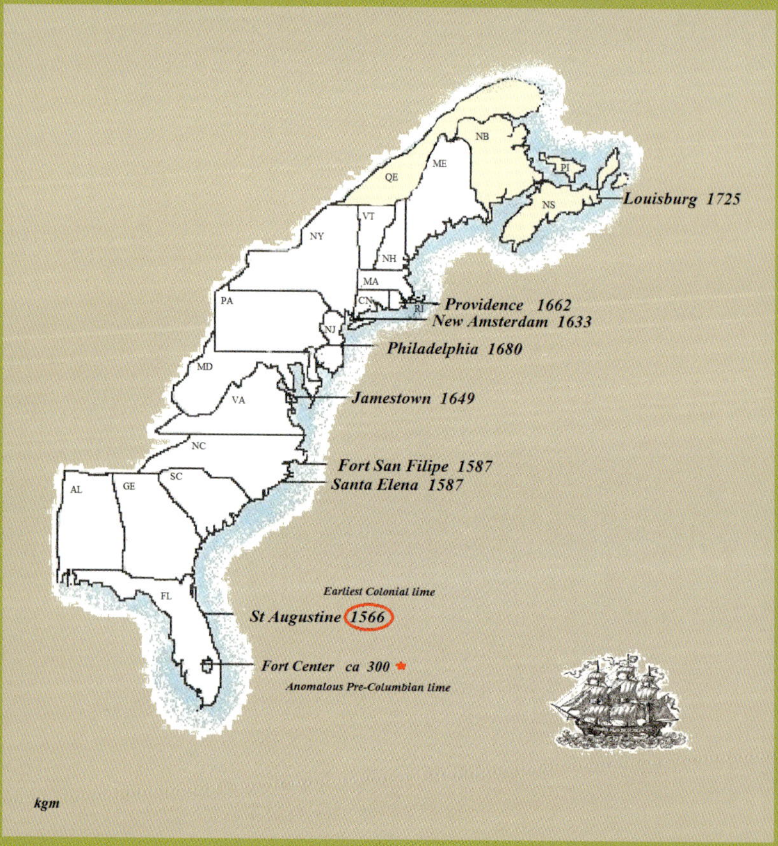

Lime Comes to America. *Digital drawing by author*

Lime Comes to America

Native Americans

The use of lime is conspicuously absent from pre-Columbian North America, given its ancient and widespread practice among the Maya and Aztec civilizations of Mesoamerica to the south. Oddly, it apparently did not extend north beyond the Rio Grande. The Pueblos built their adobe structures with "mud bricks" or stone held together and coated with mud mortar and gypsum plaster.

The "rock builders" of the Mesa Verde and Chaco Canyon traditions built their heavy stone walls with such craftsmanship and precision that only small amounts of mud plaster and wood were sufficient to hold them together for more than a thousand years. They may have used some gypsum plaster, but there is no evidence that they used lime to coat their stone and earthen floors like their southern neighbors, as well as the many ancient civilizations in the Middle East for thousands of years.

Although Native Americans did not typically use lime for architecture, some West Coast tribes apparently did produce small amounts for recreational use. While visiting the Pacific Northwest in 1787, British captain George Dixon encountered the Tlingit people. He writes, "The Indians are particularly fond of chewing a plant, which appears to be a species of tobacco; not content, however, with chewing it in its simple state, they generally mix it with lime." This habit of including a little lime when chewing tobacco, coco, or betel nut continues today in many undeveloped countries around the world (Dixon 1789).

I personally observed this habit among the Buhid tribal people living in the mountains of Mindoro, Philippines, while on sabbatical visiting missionary friends in 1985. Some of them chew betel nut, which is rolled in a grape leaf with a touch of lime, turning their mouth and saliva bright red. I am told that it produces a mild narcotic effect, and they feel that it gives them a boost of energy. One day on the trail I met this Buhid woman whose mouth was the typical bright red, but she closed her mouth tightly when I raised my camera (K. Miller, personal observation).

Florida Prairie Anomaly

In contrast, attention must be called to an anomalous example that if confirmed would represent the earliest evidence of lime in North America.

On the west side of Lake Okeechobee, in the midst of southern Florida prairie lands, is an archeological site known as Fort Center. Evidence suggests that the site was occupied by pre-Columbian people for more than 2,000 years, from before 450 BCE until about 1700 CE. It is a small, unique, and interesting site along the banks of Fisheating Creek, in the Florida savannah. Today it has blended into the landscape, with only archeologists occasionally opening the earth to verify and extend our knowledge of its past.

What makes it extremely rare is the discovery of lime there. The principal investigator, William H. Sears, describes this discovery in his book *Fort Center: An Archaeological site in the Lake Okeechobee Basin*. This seems to be of such astonishing significance that it bears quoting here:

> An unusual feature of the mound, a midden deposit, was that large quantities of lime had been made in pits by burning shells. In the floor plan, the lime pits appeared as circles. The centers of these circles were hard lime mixed with sand, which chemically approaches a fair grade of plaster. Inspection of the material under a binocular microscope demonstrates its derivation from shells; incompletely calcined shell fragments can be seen in large quantities. The "plaster" faded into a ring of shells, more thinly dispersed as one moved out from the center. Most of the shells were river mussels, but there was marine shell scrap, particularly conch and Venus clam. All of the pits excavated were used for lengthy, if variable periods of time, as shown by thin lenses of midden intruding into, at times through, the center of the lime deposits (Sears, 1994).

And so it seems that lime was indeed burned sometime between 200 and 600 CE—long before the arrival of the Europeans. The principal investigator interpreted the lime to

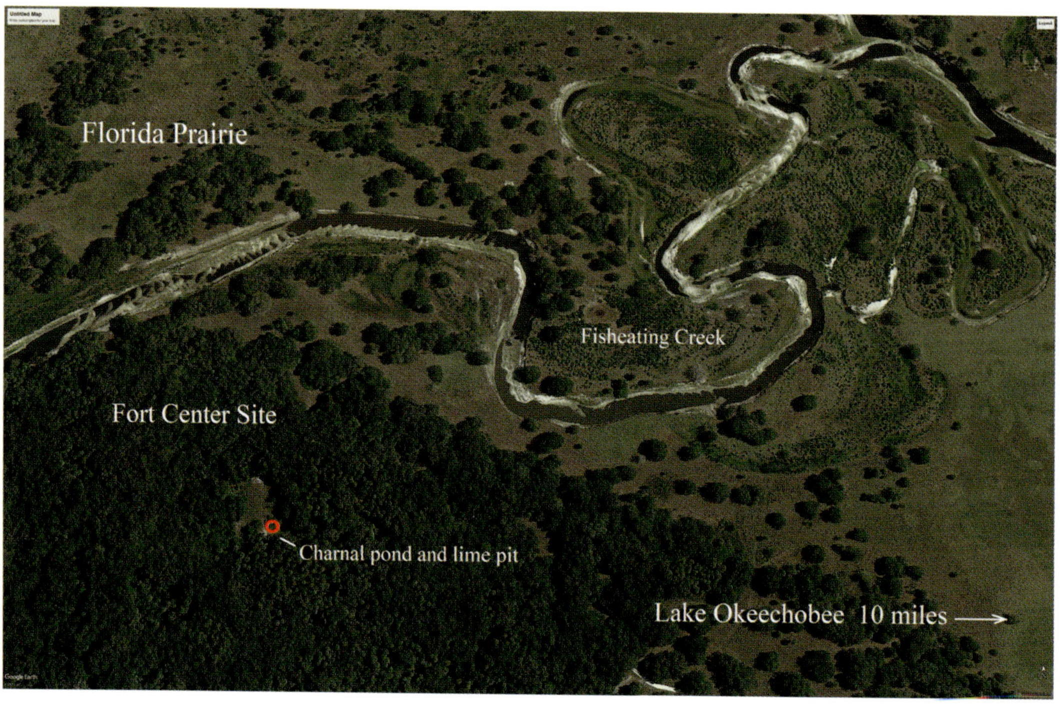

Fort Center Site, lime anomaly. *Edited from Google Earth*

Florida prairie near Fort Center. *Author*

Site of the dried-up charnel pond in 2016. The yellow circle marks the location of the excavated pit with lime remnants. *Author*

having been used on cornfields surrounded by moats. The problem with this is that corn or maize was not known to be raised by North Americans this early, and yet here at Fort Center, corn pollen was discovered in some of the moats, as well as in the lime coating on one or more wooden carvings recovered from the charnel pond at the site. Although corn was later grown by Native Americans, lime was not known to be used before being introduced by the Europeans. The presence of lime and maize at Fort Center is not known from any other pre-Columbian site and is difficult to explain.

The Earliest Colonial Lime Burning

St. Augustine

On September 8, 1565, Spanish admiral Don Pedro Menéndez de Avilés landed in Florida with a fleet of five ships (reduced from twelve in a battle with the French). Among the colonists were "some 500 soldiers, 200 seamen, and others, comprised by civilians, clergy and wives and children of 26 soldiers. All were from Spain. One hundred and thirty-eight of these soldiers also held 'office' [license] in various trades including 10 stone masons, 15 carpenters, 21 tailors, 10 shoemakers, 8 blacksmiths, 5 barbers, two surgeons, two lime makers, three swordsmiths, a gunmaker and crossbow repairman" (Deagan 2012). Menéndez immediately began to establish a settlement in the former Timucua Indian village of Seloy, naming it San Augustín (St. Augustine).

The site survived through many years of turmoil, with fort after fort being destroyed and rebuilt until Spain finally approved building a masonry fortress in 1668. Not far from the original site, construction of Castillo de San Marcos began on October 2, 1672, lasting twenty-three years.

In preparation, a large quantity of soft coquina blocks were cut from outcrops near the beach, and a large kiln was built of brick in which huge amounts of oyster shells were burned into lime. We read from a National Park Service article: "In the limekilns, oyster shells glowed white-hot and changed into fine quality, quick-setting lime. By spring of 1672, there were 4,000 *fanegas* (some 7,000 bushels) of lime in the two storehouses, and the great piles of both hewn and rough stone

Menéndez and crew surveying St. Augustine in 1565. *Image copyright purchased from Nancy Carter, Northwind Pictures Archive*

Castillo de San Marcos, St. Augustine Fort. *Author*

were a welcome sight" (National Park Service 1993).

In 1763 the magnificent fort was ceded to the British, who named it Fort St. Mark. Twenty years later it was returned to Spain. Finally, in 1821 it was ceded to the United States, first as Fort Marion, then in 1942 the original name of Castillo de San Marcos was restored. The fortress was never besieged.

Today St. Augustine is recognized as the oldest continuously occupied city in America. It is also arguably the earliest site for manufacturing lime in the colonies. An archeological team led by Dr. Kathleen Deagan discovered a circular lime-burning pit approximately 4 meters in diameter and 1.5 meters deep on the grounds of the Nuestra Señora de la Leche Shrine, adjacent to Fountain of Youth Park. It was described as being

> lined with burned pine logs, and had a flat base of charcoal. The sand under the logs and wood floor was burned to a bright red color. Layers of reduced oyster shell lime were found in the kiln, and the final load of oyster shell—as yet unburned—remained in the kiln when it was abandoned.

Radiocarbon dates indicated that the logs were felled around the turn of the fifteenth to sixteenth centuries, and the presence of artifacts suggests that the kiln was abandoned and filled in during the sixteenth century (see Deagan 2012, pp. 80–90, for a detailed discussion of this kiln).

Further evidence of this early date for lime burning is supported by historian Eugene Lyon (Lyon 1984) among papers of the Menéndez de Avilés family, who owned the site for many years; a document reads as follows:

> Described how the soldiers at the Seloy blockhouse were complaining to the authorities that they were made to burn lime, as well as guard the outpost, raising the possibility that the lime kiln and the moat at the Nombre de Dios (de Leche Shrine) site were actually related to the blockhouse left at the original Seloy town site (at the Fountain of Youth Park) which the Spaniards abandoned in 1566 in favor of Anastasia Island (Historical Archaeology).

These discoveries would make this the oldest lime kiln and earliest example of lime burning in the American colonies.

Santa Elena

After Menéndez chased the French out of Florida, in 1566 he set about establishing a settlement on the current location of Parris Island, North Carolina (on the site of the short-lived French outpost of Charlesfort), planning to relocate the capital of New Spain

Santa Elena site on Parris Island, North Carolina. *Aerial image downloaded from Google Earth*

from St. Augustine. He named it Fort San Salvador, and shortly afterward, with the arrival of reinforcements, he built a larger embattlement, renaming it Fort San Filipe, and began to establish the town of Santa Elena, which by 1569 had forty houses around a central plaza.

When the fort burned down, he built the second Fort San Filipe. The settlement was continually harassed by Indians, who eventually, in 1576, succeeded once more in burning down the fort and sacking the village. The settlers and soldiers escaped safely downriver, and Menéndez returned to Spain, where he died in 1574.

After three years the Spanish decided to again reestablish their presence on Parris Island, and in 1577, led by the new governor, Menéndez Marques (de Avilés's nephew), a new and larger garrison was erected on the island under the name Fort San Marcos. Santa Elena was rebuilt and appeared to flourish. We tell this story here because it is the next step in lime burning in the New World.

We have a record of the Spanish using lime during this second rebuilding, in a letter written from Santa Elena on March 25, 1580, to King Philip II by Governor Marques, as follows:

> This village is being very well built, and because of the method which is being followed, many of the houses appear fortified to the Indians, for they are all constructed of wood and mud, covered with lime inside and out, and with their flat roofs of lime. And as we have begun to make lime of oyster-shells, we are building in such a manner that the Indians have lost their mettle. There are more than sixty houses here, whereof thirty are of the sort I am telling your Majesty (Rowland et al. 1996; Paar 1999).

And from Lyon 1984: "When Pedro Menendez Marquez reported to the King on March 2, 1580, he could describe how far the

The British Arrive at Jamestown, depicted on this quadricentennial United States twenty-five-cent piece. *Photographed and color added by author*

rebuilding of the town of Santa Elena had progressed; now there were 60 houses, many with flat roofs of lime."

This rosy account was less than the whole story; the constant harassment by Indians, poor crop production, and the fact that a group of soldiers had commandeered a ship and left had worn the Spanish down. In 1587 the houses and fort were ordered to be demolished, and they sailed away to St. Augustine, never to return to Santa Elena.

Jamestown

After a number of failed attempts, beginning in 1586 the British eventually established a permanent colony at Jamestown, Virginia, in 1607. The settlement had a rocky history as a result of draught, starvation, Indian raids, and incompetence. Less than half the settlers between 1608 and 1624 survived, but the British persisted. More than once, when the colony was about to collapse, recruitments and supplies arrived from England just in time, and Jamestown survived to become the capitol of Virginia Colony for one hundred years, after which, in 1699, it was relocated to Williamsburg. The town of Jamestown survived another fifty years before being largely abandoned.

From the very beginning of the British arrival, tradesmen of all sorts were included on the ships' passenger lists. They were clearly planning to stay and build with brick, and that would require lime for mortar. According to historian J. Paul Hudson:

> Contemporary records reveal that "lyme burners" emigrated to Jamestown as early as 1610. As four lime kilns were found during excavations, it is evident that the lime that was used by the Jamestown builders was made on the historical island. In the kilns oyster shells from the James River were burned and converted into lime by the limeburners (Hudson 1957).

Hudson may be referring to a document in Brown 1819 titled "*CLXIII. Classes of Immigrants Wanted, The Trades-men to be sent into Virginia under comaunde of Sir Thomas Gates*," which was likely circulated in 1610, prior to Gate's voyage. It contains a list of more than three hundred souls representing more than sixty-six different trades, including four brickmakers, six bricklayers, and two "lyme burners" (Hudson 1957).

The first temporary dwellings in the settlement are believed to have resembled the bark-covered, bent-sapling huts of the Indians, but with timber being plentiful, the houses were soon erected around a framework of posts dug into the ground. The spaces between were filled in with reeds, mud, and plaster, or possibly rude brickwork ("brick-noggin" or nogging). Some soon replaced the "earthbound" foundations with brick pillars and eventually brick foundations, and brick replaced the wood and daub chimneys.

In Shaw 1930, we find the following reference to bricks and lime attributed to a letter to him from historian Ellis Lovejoy. He says:

> The first mention of brickmaking I can find is in 1611 when Sir Thomas Dale arrived. He set the colonists to work building additions to James town and making needed repairs and among other things at "making brick" I could find no use of these bricks in Jamestown, but later in 1611 Dale with 200 men built the town of Henrico up the river from Jamestown. Among the men were potters, brick-makers, and brick-layers, besides smiths . . . "three streets of well framed houses, a handsome church, and the foundations for a more stately one laid in bricks, in length an hundred foot and fiftie foot wide." . . . "The bricks were made from the coastal plains clay and such clays require a high temperature to burn—around cone 10. They were burned in scoved kilns and the lime made from oyster shells was burned in the kiln with the bricks, likely in top of the kiln (Shaw 1930).

According to Samuel Yonge, the first brick house of the colony was built in 1638, and the first brick church in 1639–1647. In 1642 Sir William Berkley, the new governor, arrived, bearing instructions from the royal government to rebuild the town with brick houses, which was begun, but in 1676 the entire town was destroyed (Yonge 1904).

In 1724 Hugh Jones writes in *The Present State of Virginia*:

> The first Metropolis, James Town, was built in the most convenient Place for Trade and Security against the Indians, but often received much damage, being twice burned down; after which it never recovered its Perfection, consisting at present of nothing but Abundance of Brick Rubbish, and three or four, good inhabited Houses, tho' the Parish is of pretty large Extent, but less than others (Jones 1724; reprinted in Jones 2018).

In 1626 Abraham Peirsey built his "brick-nogged" home resting on a siltstone foundation west of Jamestown. And in the 1630s, Capt. Samuel Matthews built "Mathews Manor" east of Jamestown, a two-story Elizabethan "nogged farmhouse" resting on a two-brick-wide foundation. The first all-brick house in Virginia was built in 1638 by Secretary Richard Kemp. A partially brick church was begun in Jamestown in 1639; it later burned and was replaced by a more substantial building in 1676, the ruins of which may be seen today (Brown 1998).

Many houses of the common farmer continued to be built of wood. An interesting description of colonial houses in 1686 appears in a little book written by one French Huguenot, Durand de Dauphine, as follows:

> There are some very good houses in this country. Those of the peasants are all of wood. They are sheathed with chestnut plank and sealed inside with the same. As they get ahead in the world they refinish the interior with plaster, for which they use oyster shell lime, making it white as snow; so that although the houses seem poor enough on the outside because one sees only the weathered sheathing, within they are most agreeable. Most of the houses are amply pierced with glazed windows. They make great quantities of brick in Virginia and I saw a number of houses built entirely of brick (Durand de Dauphine 1687).

These early foundations and chimneys, and houses of brick and stone, required lime for mortar. The first lime from Florida to New England was made by burning oyster shells, which were found in abundance in middens along the coast. Not long after the establishment of Philadelphia, vast deposits of limestone were discovered just west of the city, and this site then provided most of the lime from there on.

Lime in New Amsterdam, 1609–1642

The Dutch presence in the colonies began in 1609, when Capt. Henry Hudson sailed the *Half Moon* up the river that was to take on his name. Although searching for a "Northwest Passage" for the Dutch East Indian Company, his venture instead led to the establishment of a trading post at what is today Albany, New York, and a patent from the States General granting a trade monopoly for the territory between the 38th and 45th parallels.

The first settlers established themselves on Manhattan Island near the mouth of the river, where in 1628 a fort of scaled-down proportions, with walls of mud and sand, was built. Peter Minuit became the Dutch West Indian director general of New Amsterdam. In 1642 the new governor, William Kieft, had a large stone house built at the Coenties Slip on the west side of Pearl Street. It was called "Stadt Huys," a tavern serving as the first city hall as well (Davis 1854). Lime would have been required in its building.

He also had a large stone church built within the fort in 1642:

> A contract was drawn up in May, 1642, setting forth an agreement between Governor William Kieft, Gilbert op Dyck, and Thomas Willet, of New Amsterdam to build a stone church within the fort. . . . Indian wars retarded building the church which was not finished in 1654, but in due time the steep double pointed roof arose over the walls of the fort. . . . Stone was ferried ashore near the fort, the wardens agreeing to carry the stone from the shore to the fort, and to furnish lime with which to lay them (Wheeler 1907).

New England

Limestone was discovered in Rhode Island about 1660, in northern Massachusetts in 1697, and at Thomaston, Maine, about 1730 (Garvin 2002).

Rhode Island

By the 1730s, lime production in Rhode Island had become an important, expanding industry. In colonial days, all the lime produced was made from oyster shells. Here in New England, limestone appears in pockets close inland from the coast. These deposits were apparently first exploited near Providence in about 1661.

The Providence *Early Records of Lime Rock, Rhode Island* states that on January 27, 1662, one Thomas Hackelton, "making his request unto the Towne ___ have liberty to burne lime upon the Comonneere about ____ and to take stones and wood for the same purpose" [spaces absent in reference, Providence Early Records 3.8; Rider 1904]

Massachusetts

The first limestone quarry and kiln in Massachusetts is reported by John J. Currier as follows:

> The limestone at this locality was discovered by Ensign James Noyes, and worked beginning in 1697, the first "lime quarry" in colonial Massachusetts. Before this time lime used for mortar for construction purposes was derived from oyster and clam shells. In his diary, under date of Sept. 8, 1697, volume 5, page 458, Judge Sewal gives an account of "the body of limestone discovered at Newbury." The town also voted that "the kiln for burning said lime shall be built at or near the end of Muzzie's lane, next to the Merrimac River" (Currier 1896).

New Hampshire

Relatively small amounts of limestone were found in ledges throughout New Hampshire; namely, at Plainfield, Lyme, Oxford, Haverhill (1838), Lyman, Littleton, and elsewhere. "In 1837 limestone was discovered at the base of

Sugarloaf Mountain in the White Mountains where Chester Spooner built the first kiln, and large amounts of limestone on Black Mountain Pike in 1842 where William Garrett built a second kiln" (Hitchcock 1874).

Maine

Although small amounts of limestone may be found throughout the "Pine Tree State," nearly all of Maine's industrial limestone has come from Knox County, where it is found in narrow, deep deposits near the coast in a 12-mile stretch from Camden through Rockport and Rockland to Thomaston, which until recently was the center of lime manufacturing on the East Coast.

Lime was discovered here in 1732 by Samuel Waldo, who had secured a grant of land from King Charles and founded the colony Waldoboro (Finch and Howe 1930). It was produced and exported to Boston as early as 1733 by Gen. Henry Knox, George Washington's undersecretary of war, who had settled at Thomaston after the Revolution and developed a major lime-manufacturing industry.

Philadelphia

William Penn sailed from England with a group of colonists on the *Welcome* on August 30, 1682. They arrived at the mouth of the Delaware Bay on October 24 and continued upriver on a three-day journey to the Dutch settlement of Newcastle. This settlement was now a part of Penn's grant, and he was openly welcomed by the Dutch and Swedish settlers, receiving title from the Duke of York's agents.

Penn then continued upriver 18 miles to Upland, which he promptly named Chester. The next day he was rowed another 16 miles upriver past the Schuylkill, landing at the mouth of Dock Creek and the "Sign of the Blue Anchor" log tavern. The tavern would have seen frequent travelers, with some fifty Europeans in the area living among the Native American Lenni Lenape people, and ships passing by upriver to Burlington, on the eastern shore of the Delaware.

Upon arrival, the colonists immediately set about constructing rude huts and "caves" cut into the bank along the river. The plan for the city of Philadelphia was laid out by Penn before he arrived, and log houses quickly began to appear on rectangular lots within the city. Even the lime would have been used as plaster chinking or mortar in brick or stone foundations. We read of mortar from the very beginning in Dixon 1851:

> Delicate women, used to all the luxuries in England, went out to help their fathers and husbands; they brought in wood and water; they cooked with their own hands; . . . some

THE LANDING OF PENN AT DOCK CREEK PENNA

Penn's Landing at Dock Creek. Digital painting by the author; modified after an anonymous painting in the Pennsylvania State Museum Library

> of them acted as laborers while the house was building, anxious to carry mortar, or lend a hand to saw a block of wood.

Although there is considerable literature regarding building with brick in these early days, there is very little mention of the lime that would have been needed for mortar. They obviously burned lime for this purpose, although we must wait until 1685, when it is mentioned in a letter from Robert Turner to William Penn in England. It reads, in part, "Samuel Carpenter is our lime burner on his Wharf. Brave Lime Stone found here, as the Workmen say, being proved" (Turner 1685).

Timber-framed houses with brick panels (nogging) preceded those built entirely of brick. The following excerpt likely refers to the "Blue Anchor Tavern":

> The first place completed was used as a tavern, a ferry house, and a general place of business. . . . This important building was formed of large rafters of wood, the interstices being filled with bricks brought from England, in the manner of Cheshire houses of the Tudor and Stuart periods (Dixon 1851).

Penn felt strongly about building with brick, and, in short time, bricks were manufactured and began replacing logs. Brick chimneys, brick foundations and cellars, and nogging soon gave way to entire houses of brick. There is considerable disagreement regarding the "first brick house" in Pennsylvania, but it was likely built sometime around 1683. The following may be a few candidates.

Letitia House (1682). The brick house standing in Fairmont Park—sometimes referred to as the Letitia House—has a sign over the door: "Home of William Penn, built 1682; Moved to this place, 1883," a claim that is now discounted. It is possible Penn lived in the building for a time when it was near the waterfront, although this is also disputed.

Friend's Meeting House in Chester (1682). The First General Assembly met upon Penn's arrival in "the most commodious building in Chester, the Friend's Meeting House, a plain brick edifice, fronting the Creek, and opposite to Wade's House, where Penn remained a guest" (Dixon 1851).

Regarding Pennsbury Manor (1683)—Penn's three-story brick mansion— Luke Torrance writes in the *Bucks County Courier Times*:

> Construction of the original house began in 1683, shortly after Penn arrived in the Americas to oversee his new colony. Penn moved into the house a few years later and split his time between the country estate, a residence in Philadelphia and his home in England for the next 15 years. In 1701, he left Pennsylvania for the final time—debt and illness prevented his return. He died in 1718 in England (Torrance 2017).

James Claypool House (1684). One of Penn's confidants, James Claypool arrived in Philadelphia on October 6, 1683, and the following spring (1684) built a "proper" house, reputedly the first of brick in Philadelphia. "It was a double two-story brick house, had four leaden-framed windows in front, and the same in the rear . . . with a beautiful south exposure, down a descending green into the pleasant Dock Creek" (Brunk 2002).

Robert Turner House (1684). A wealthy merchant from Dublin and one of Penn's major land holders, he also built a brick house that same year. "In 1863 Turner made his home in Philadelphia, and engaged in a flourishing mercantile business. During the summer of 1684 he erected the first brick house in Philadelphia, located at the corner of First and Mulberry (Arch) Streets. In the same year Daniel Pegge, a future brother-in-law of Richard's, had a brick house built in 'Pegge's Run'" (Smith 2013).

FIVE

Into the Wilderness.
Digital drawing by the author

Into the Wilderness

Arrival of the Palatines

Early Friday morning, June 24, 1710—as recorded by H. Frank Eshleman—the *Maria Hope*, a small sailing ship, hauled out of London loaded with ninety-four passengers. Aboard were six Swiss Mennonite men who would form the nucleus of the first permanent settlement along the Pequea Creek in Lancaster County. There is no mention of their families, though we would assume that they were included. After a fair journey of ninety-two days, they arrived at Philadelphia in September 1710 (Eshleman 1969).

Little is known of their activities during that first year in this new land. There would have been friends and relatives established at Germantown, and it is likely that some of them spent that first winter there. No doubt some of the men soon set out to explore the land that was warranted to them, shortly after their arrival. That warrant is described in brief:

> Ten thousand acres of land with reasonable allowances for roads and highways on the northwest side of a hill about twenty miles easterly from Conestoga and near the head of Pequea Creek.

Immigrants arriving at Philadelphia in the early eighteenth century. *Photo by the author of a "3-D painting" by Aaron Zook, on display at the Lancaster Mennonite Historical Society, 2215 Millstream Road, Lancaster, Pennsylvania, and used here with their permission*

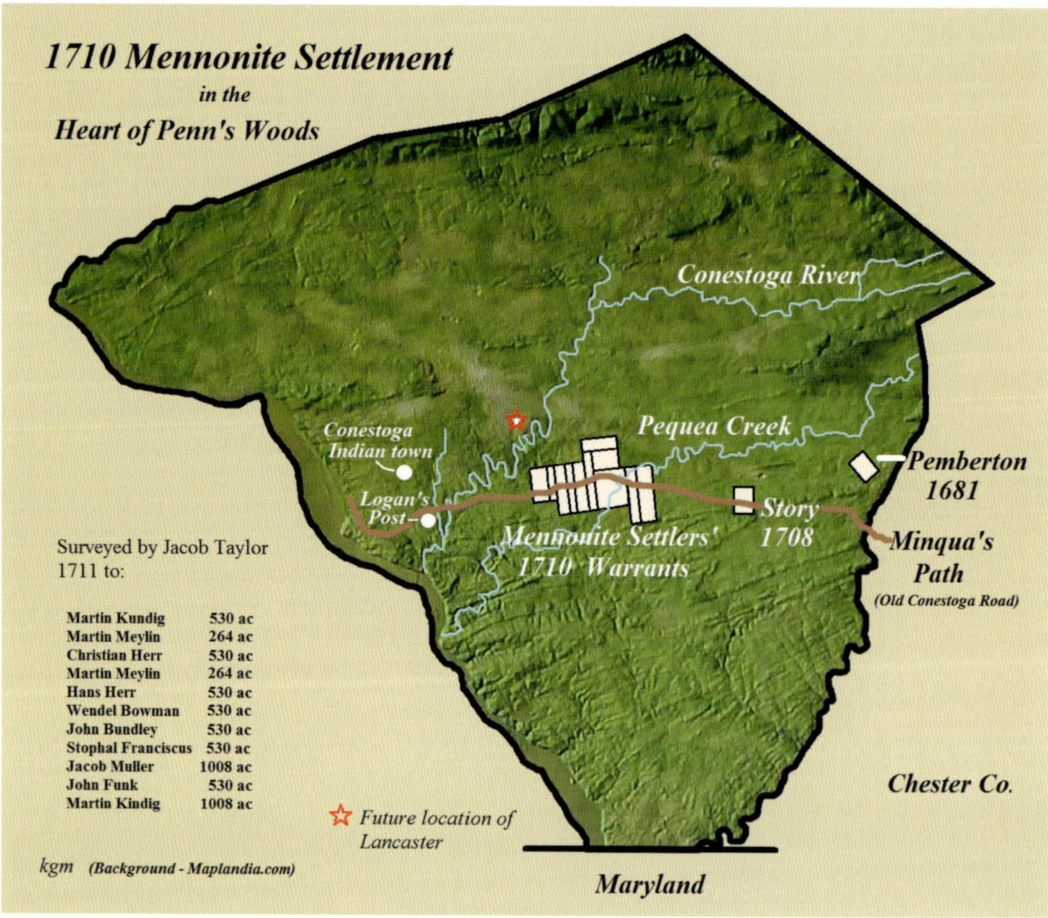

Draft of the 10,000-acre Mennonite settlement of 1710 along Pequea Creek, near the present-day towns of Strasburg and Willow Street, Pennsylvania. *Digitally overlain on a Google Earth map by the author*

We don't know how that particular site was selected. This description doesn't match the site that was later surveyed and where they eventually settled. The phrase "twenty miles easterly" would place the tract in the vicinity of New Holland, the Welsh Mountains, and the origin of the Pequea Creek. On the other hand, the tract that was surveyed and settled is near Pequea Creek in the vicinity of present-day Strasburg and Willow Street.

By the following summer, we read that the small band of immigrants was reported to be settled with their families at Pequea; we have this information from a meeting with the Indians at Conestoga on June 13, 1711. At this meeting the governor inquired about the "Palatines settled on Pequea," to which the Indians replied, "As to the Palatines they are in our opinion safely seated." It is assumed that on arrival they threw together temporary shelters of sailcloth, branches, and brush and worked at putting up more-substantial log cabins on their individual tracts. In any case, Eshleman quotes from a letter by Jacob Taylor, Penn's surveyor, to James Logan on July 20, 1711, in which he says, "six or seven families are settled at Pequea" (Eshleman 1969).

Of Logs and Lime

C. Henry Smith writes on the Pequea Colony in *The Mennonites of America*:

This old log building overlooks Pequea Creek less than a mile south of the original Mennonite settlement. *Photo by the author, reversed for composition*

> Travelling about sixty miles out of Philadelphia they reached a rich limestone region along the banks of the Pequea, in what was then Chester, but now Lancaster County. Here they decided to put up their first log cabins." (Smith 1909).

The log cabin is the quintessential symbol of the American frontier, which at that time included the forests and glades of Lancaster County. It is the simplest of structures, built like a box by using logs that were cut while the settlers were clearing the surrounding forests.

The practice of building houses by laying up horizontal logs has had a long tenure, originating in northern Europe many hundreds of years ago and brought to North America by the Swedes and Germans in the mid-seventeenth century. For the next two hundred years it was the basic house of the pioneers as

Dovetail corners and remains of whitewash on an old log house in southern Lancaster County. The whitewash was preserved under a covering of siding. *Photo by the author*

they moved south into the mountains of Virginia, west to the Rio Grande, and north into the Yukon and Alaskan wilderness. There is almost nowhere in this great land where there was not once a log cabin.

As trees were felled, they were debarked, occasionally were hewn "square," and then were laid one atop the other, notched at the ends and overlapping in the manner of children's "Lincoln Logs." Holes for small windows and doors were cut in and a hearth or large fireplace was built, with the chimney exiting near the middle of the house, unlike the English, who built their fireplaces on the ends of the house. Bits of wood bark, stones, grass, and moss were packed into the gaps between the logs and then reinforced with mud.

If lime was available, it was used to reinforce this chinking, to strengthen the foundation, to lay up the stones of a fireplace and chimney, and to make plaster and whitewash to protect, strengthen, and brighten up wooden and stone surfaces, inside and out, and to freshen the stables and coat the fences.

Stone Houses

The 1719 Hans Herr House

After living in his log house for about eight years, Christian Herr decided to build larger. This one would be of stone. It would be the

This beautifully restored "1719 Hans Herr House" is on Hans Herr Drive, approximately half a mile due east of the village of Willow Street, Pennsylvania. *Photo by the author*

first stone house in the settlement and almost certainly Lancaster County. According to tradition, it would be a fitting residence for himself and his father, Hans—both religious leaders in the community—and it would also serve as the meeting house for this first Mennonite community. On the stone above the front entrance, today we find "17 CHHR 19," a carving that has survived three centuries and is today the oldest surviving masonry building in the county, now wonderfully restored by the Mennonite Historical Society as an historical site representative of a small colonial plantation.

Christian may have considered it modest, and today it does look small, sitting in the open grounds. It actually has more than 2,500 square feet of floor space, nearly the average size of many houses in the United States today.

Although we have no records of its actual construction, it would in all likelihood have been a community project, with various neighboring craftsman taking part. Christian also had his hands in the construction, leaving his initials pressed into the mortar on the

The initials of Christian Herr pressed into the original lime plaster in the upper floor of the 1719 Hans Herr House. *Photo by the author*

chimney of the second floor.

We can't help but wonder where the lime for the mortar, plaster, and whitewash came from. A considerable amount of lime was being produced in the Philadelphia area at this time, and it is possible a few barrels may have been brought from there, but with limestone everywhere under their feet, it is reasonable to assume that these resourceful pioneers would have put to use the lime-burning skills they brought with them from their home country. Quite likely they burned the lime on the grounds, no doubt in a pit kiln.

The following article describing such a temporary "pit kiln" appeared in the *Country Gentleman* on November 11, 1869 (Stewart 1869):

> Editors Country Gentleman . . . A common mode among Pennsylvania farmers of burning lime for their own use is by means of "pits." . . . To make a pit: Lay off a piece of ground, say 16 feet square, more or less as may be needed; build up a wall of large pieces of limestone round the plot, leaving a draft hole on each side, from which make an air-way of large pieces to the centre; by these air-ways the draft can be regulated to moderate or increase the fire.
>
> Build a foundation of cord wood or rough logs, laid in with small wood, that may fire easily; throw on a layer of stone a foot and a half thick; then wood and stone alternately, taking care to build up the outer wall as solidly as possible, so that it may not fall in as the burning mass may settle down; and make the wall to taper a little, as it is carried up, to effect this purpose better.
>
> When the pile is taken up as high as needed, cover up with small stone and chips from the quarry to confine the heat; plaster over the outside with clay, filling in the cracks between the stones with moss, grass, hay, or coarse manure, or anything that will prevent access of air, which should be admitted only by the draft holes at the bottom.
>
> When well on fire close these holes almost entirely, and keep them so regulated so as to maintain a constant, moderate heat. If the stone is a pure crystalline limestone, it should burn three or four days; if flinty or what is called by quarrymen "dry stone," it will take a week or more to calcine sufficiently; experience, however, is the best guide in this particular.
>
> A magnesium limestone or "dolomite" makes an excellent "land" lime, though a poor building lime, and most of the highly crystalline limestone is of this character; it requires to be well but slowly burnt. . . . Henry Stewart, Stroudsburg, Pa.

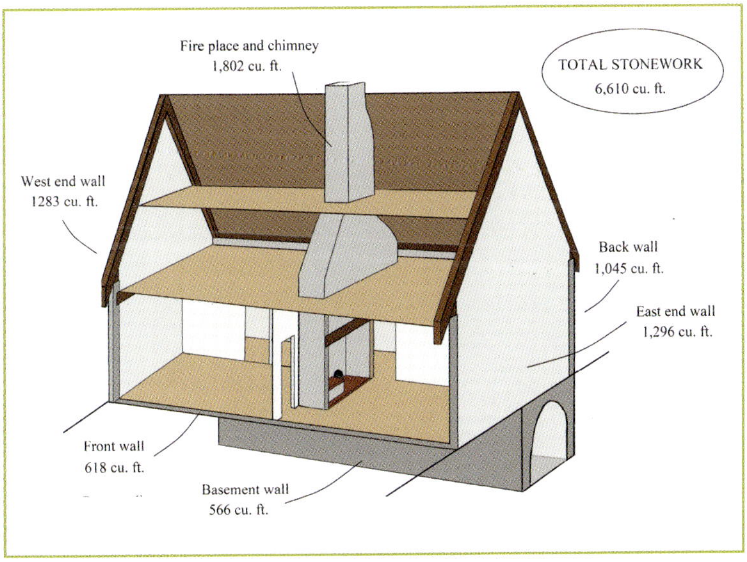

Open schematic showing the approximate cubic feet of stonework in the building

Conestoga wagon and team. *Digital painting by the author*

Lime for the Hans Herr House

The first stone house in Lancaster County was built upon an outcrop of solid sandy limestone, from which the stone for the building was also excavated. The mortar for its construction required a considerable amount of lime. How much, we wondered? With a measuring tape, notebook, computer, and access to architectural reconstruction records (Milner 1972), we were able to create this "opened up" view (*shown*). This illustration helps visualize the masonry portions of the structure—the four outside walls, the internal fireplace and chimney, and the basement walls—and in calculating the total cubic feet of stone wall making up the building.

While there are a great many variables involved, from several old references we estimated that 202 pounds (or 2.65 bushels) of lime will build 100 cubic feet (1 cord) of stone wall (Morris 1900; Arthur 1914).

We calculated that the Herr House contains approximately 6,610 cubic feet of stonework in the walls, fireplace, and chimney, requiring 12,342 pounds of lime, plus the amount needed for interior plaster (1,722 pounds), thus totaling 14,064 pounds, or roughly 7 tons.

The stone for building was obtained on the site, but in the wilderness of 1719, where does one obtain 7 tons of lime? Lacking such records, we might speculate on four different sources.

Lime-burning stack, with cutaway showing internal layers of wood and stone. *Digital painting by the author*

Lime-burning pit with cutaway showing stone piled on the wood fire. *Digital painting by the author*

- Philadelphia. As early as 1686, Madam Farmer was burning lime at her estate along the Schuylkill River north of Philadelphia, and by 1714 the Great Conestoga Road was running through the Hans Herr tract on its way to Rock Hill, where James Logan had his trading station on the West Branch. In 1717 he purchased a Conestoga wagon to haul furs and other items to Philadelphia and return with supplies for the settlers (*Journal of Lancaster County's Historical Society* 57 [1953]). These massive wagons are reported to carry up to 6 tons or more and would have been able to deliver many barrels of lime almost to Christian Herr's front door. Considering the cost, and the fact that limestone was everywhere underfoot, it is more likely that these industrious pioneers would put to work the practice they were familiar with from the "old country."
- A lime kiln. For the task of burning lime, the settlers of the Pequea community may have gotten together to build a lime kiln for their mutual use. This would have been done in time, but there are other simpler methods of burning lime that were more likely used.
- A stack. This method was widely used in this area during the nineteenth century, although records are lacking for the colonial period. Although involving a lot of work, a stack could be thrown up near the construction site.
- A lime pit. This is the simplest and oldest way to make lime. It was widely used in Britain, and far back into the history of lime burning in the Middle East and elsewhere. A relatively shallow pit 4 or 5 feet deep could easily be dug, preferably into a slope, possibly lined with stone, then piled with logs and branches and filled to a mound with broken limestone. Several openings around the bottom would allow for a regulated draft, and the whole might be covered with sod or soil. The fuel would be ignited and burned for several days to a week or more, until the limestone was completely calcined. As it burned, the entire mass would collapse into the pit. Water might be added to slack the quicklime into a slurry right on the spot.

Whatever the source of lime, the Hans Herr House was the first of many stone homes that were built to replace the original log houses throughout Lancaster County and beyond.

1719 Hans Herr House, summer 2018. *Author*

SIX

The Lime Kilns of Lancaster County

This bucolic scene along the Conestoga River a mile and a half south of Millersville, Pennsylvania, shows a herd of Holstein cows peacefully grazing near a lime kiln in "Ken Shertzer's Meadow." *Author*

Following the Limestone

The Lancaster County landscape has been attracting the eye of visitors for more than three centuries. In 1710 Swiss/German immigrants had to travel no more than 60 miles west from the port of Philadelphia to find some of the best limestone soil in the world. Here, half a dozen families chose to settle the first 10,000 acres along the banks of the Pequea to carve out of Penn's Woods a new land and a new life.

The colony grew rapidly, as these courageous pioneers were immediately followed by shiploads of friends and relatives, many of them fellow Mennonites who had been hounded from their homeland in central Europe for refusing to surrender their strong religious values and unwelcome beliefs.

Renowned as farmers, they also brought with them valuable skills as artisans and tradesmen and a strong work ethic, accompanied by a strict sense of family and religious conviction. They set to work clearing the woods of the massive oaks, hickories, and chestnuts and turning forests into productive farmland. It is said they watched for black locust trees, a signal that there was good limestone beneath their roots.

The land they chose was in the midst of a broad valley or plain with thousands of square miles of this limestone, gentle hills, primeval forest, well-watered meadows, and a favorable climate. Here, in a few short generations, they turned their "Palatine Paradise" into the "Garden Spot of the World."

Limestone was the key. Not only does it generate a productive, rich loamy soil, but

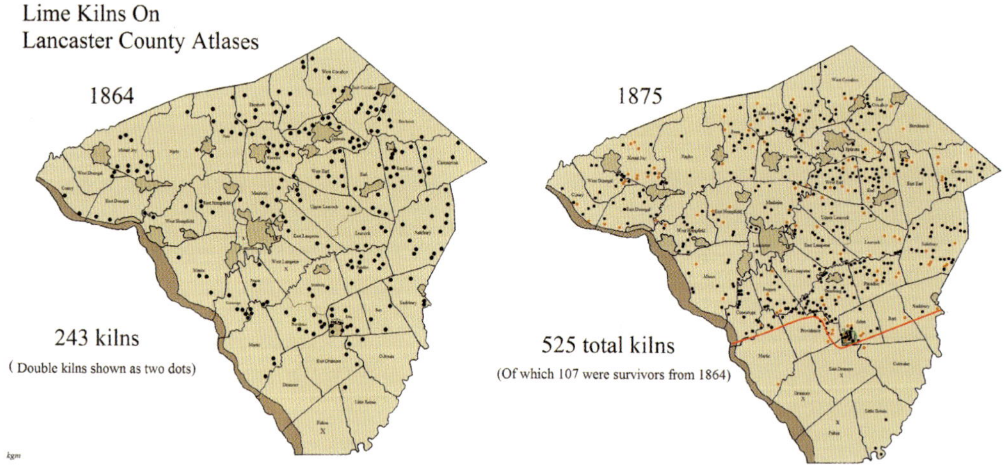

Lime kilns identified on the 1864 and 1875 county atlases. *Drawn and plotted by the author*

when quarried it yields ideal building material, such as pictured on the lime kiln overlooking the bucolic meadow (*above*). Just as locust trees indicated good soil to the pioneers, a generation later, lime kilns would be the sign of productive farmland.

In 1754, Thomas Pownall, who would become governor of the Massachusetts Bay Colony, paid a visit to this area and later wrote:

> Pequea affords a pleasant prospect—a rich landscape—farmhouses surrounded with apple and peach trees. The farmers, proprietors, not tenants. On every farm a lime-kiln, and the land adapted for the best of wheat (Conyingham 1842).

We find no records telling us about that first lime kiln in Lancaster County, but surely it would have been within the "Mennonite settlement" on the banks of the Pequea, not far from Mary Faree's home in Strasburg, or within sight of the 1719 Hans Herr House, the first stone house built in the community by Christian Herr, for which lime would have been essential to make mortar, plaster, and whitewash.

True to the biblical admonition "Be fruitful and multiply," all the tillable land of the county was quickly converted to farmland. The first large plantations were later divided among sons and daughters, and the number of farms increased, occupying every "nook and cranny" where crops could be made to grow. Ten generations and more have now earned their living while diligently tilling this valuable land.

It is not uncommon to find many scenes like the Shertzer farm (*above*), with its quaint old lime kiln silently keeping watch over the well-bred cows that patiently graze the lush green grass of their tranquil meadow.

A Past Record of Lime Kilns

County Atlases

Written records of individual rural lime kilns in Lancaster County are virtually nonexistent. Interestingly and fortunately, both *Bridgens' Atlas of Lancaster Co., Penna.* (Bridgens 1864) and Everts & Stewart's *Combination Atlas Map of Lancaster County, Pennsylvania* (Everts & Stewart 1875) have lime kilns marked. There are other old maps of the county, but these are the only two that mark the kilns. In 1855, H. F. Bridgens published a map titled *The Three Earls*, which does mark the lime kilns, but it covers only three townships: Earl, East Earl,

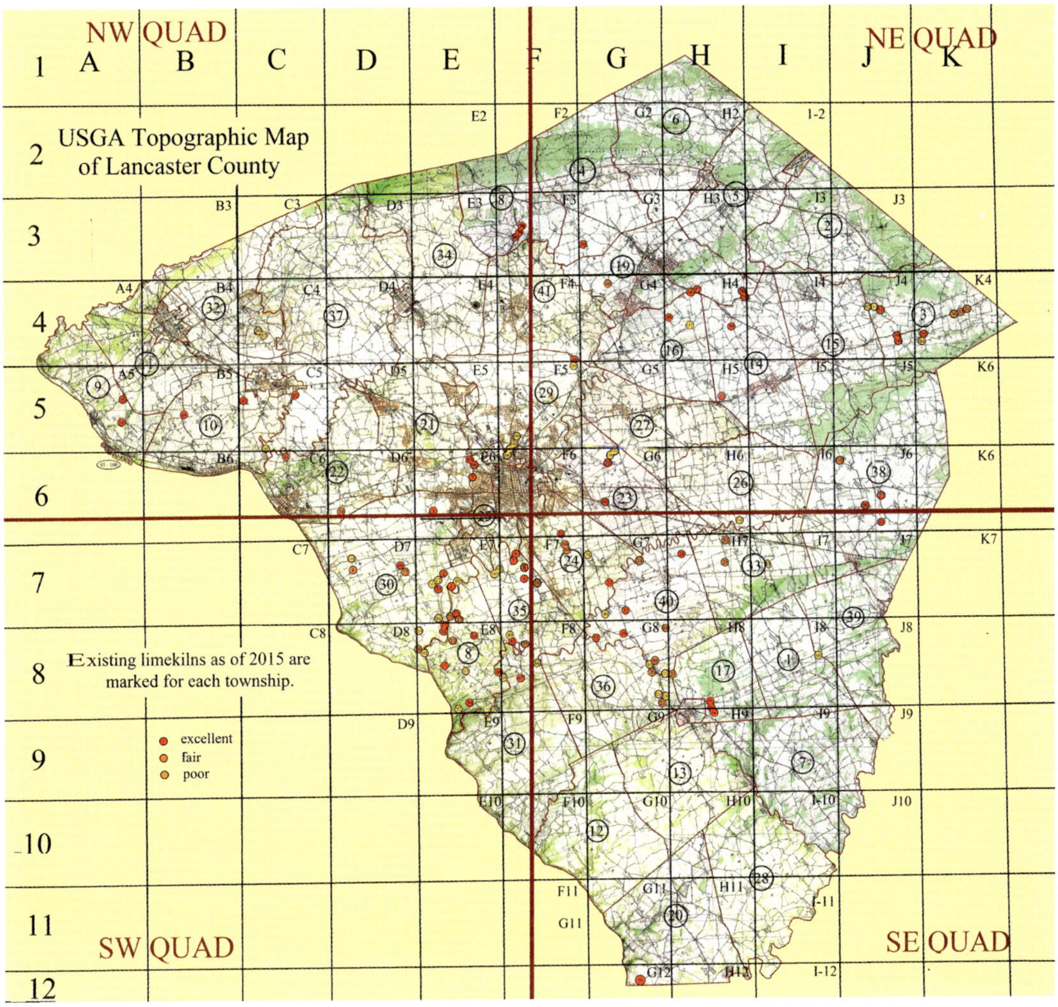

Locations of Lancaster County's extant lime kilns. *Plotted on a composite topographic map of Lancaster County townships by the author*

and West Earl. The few copies that I have seen are tattered, brown, and hard to read.

The locations of the kilns on the above maps are about as accurate as can be done with this size of formatting. For more precision, see the individual maps on the kiln photo pages, which show each township in detail. Full-size topographic (topo) maps are available at most libraries and museums in the county, as well as online, though the online maps are photocopied in black and white and are less than sharp.

Note on these maps how the number of kilns more than doubled in about ten years. Several factors would have been at work. The population of the county grew from approximately 18,000 to 23,000 during this time, while the number of farms in the county increased by approximately 50 percent between 1850 and 1880, growing from a farm population of 6,175 to 9,070.

Farming was a good business to get into; farms were divided up among children. More land was being cleared on each farm, increasing the tillage per farm, all of which led to an increase in the demand for lime as a soil amendment and for mortar, plaster, whitewash, and cement around farms and elsewhere. For the time being, many farmers chose to burn their own lime from stone on their farms, but by the turn of the century (1900), commercial lime-manufacturing enterprises were being spawned throughout the county.

This development led to disuse and neglect of old lime kilns, whose use required a lot of labor, trees, and coal. Lime could now be fetched by a team from a commercial producer not far away. Additionally, the availability of mixed chemical fertilizers and Portland cement led to the virtual abandonment of the rural lime kiln on the farm. Few lasted beyond the first decade of the twentieth century. Unfortunately, we don't have details or maps to document this phenomenon after 1875.

Lancaster County Survey (2017)

This composite topographic map of Lancaster County (p. 67) shows the location of the 128 lime kilns identified in this study. The inventory in the appendix ranks them according to their condition, from 10 down to as low as 0.2. On this map they are color coded, with red being good (10 to 7), orange being fair (6 to 4), and yellow being poor (3 to 0.2).

The Survey

Historical information about each kiln is virtually nonexistent. Surprisingly, no one has recorded much about these ancient monuments of "Pennsylvania Dutch" agricultural history. Oral history is even worse. I talked with a great many farmers who had lime kilns on their land and knew almost nothing about that lime kiln out there along the woods. Of course it has been two or three generations since the old lime kiln was used, and farms often have changed hands several times during that period. Many farmers would know it's a lime kiln, but they often ask, "How did those things work?"

A typical response came from an old Amish farmer who had owned the farm for about fifty years. When asked whether he knew anything about his kiln, he paused thoughtfully and answered, "No . . . chust came with the farm."

Lime kilns are transient things and come and go over the years as needed. None of the kilns on the 1875 atlas maps may be found today. Many want to know "When was it built?" Something that I would like to have known myself. Of all the kilns on the county map, there is only one that has a date: Kiln No. 62, one of a set of three attached kilns hidden in the woods near Quarryville. It has the date June 7, 1879, carved on a large stone on the front wall. Undoubtedly that was the date it was built. (A picture of the date stone is shown in the Quarryville Kilns section of chapter 7).

Approximate dates may be estimated by examining the 1864 and 1875 county atlases, which include a wealth of information on the township maps, including kilns and quarries. Kilns are marked as a circle with a dot in the center, and quarries as a small arc with short parallel lines, as noted on the small section from Eden Township in the 1875 atlas. Not all of the draftsmen were consistent, and occasionally a dot may be missing from the circle. If this circle is close to a quarry it is quite likely a kiln. Sometimes these circles are labeled as LK, or even "lime kiln" and "quarry." Taking these things into consideration, we can assume a small margin of error in our inventory counts for those years. Nevertheless, if a kiln is marked on the 1875 atlas but not on the 1864, we can assume it was likely built sometime within that approximately ten-year span.

As seen in the Inventory of Lime Kilns in Lancaster table in the appendix, approximately 135 kilns, ruins, and remains have been documented and photographed within Lancaster County (depending on how they are counted). Most of the kilns have a single pot and arch. Some may have two arches, which may or may not have been built as a unit at the same time. Commercial kilns such as Billmeyer and Belmont have rows of kilns. In this survey we counted each arch and pot as one kiln.

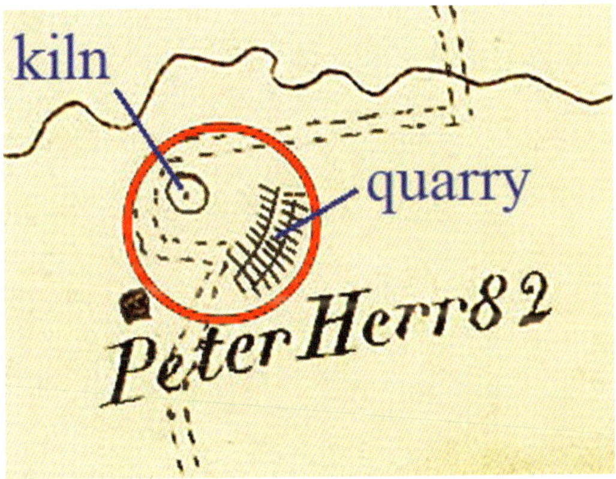

Enlargement showing Peter Herr's kiln near the top left of the map

"No . . . chust came with the farm." *Cartoon commissioned by local artist Richard Weidman*

A section from the 1875 Lancaster County atlas, showing locations of lime kilns near Strasburg. *Red circles drawn by author for emphasis*

Lime Kiln Arch Styles

Although the working design of all kilns is basically the same, each one is unique. Some kilns are constructed of limestone, others of sandstone or fieldstone, depending on what is locally available. Their uniqueness is never more evident than in the style of the front arch, which must support the heavy stones above it, a feat accomplished by the various designs shown. Some are curved like a Roman arch, with many variations, while others are flat, with the upper part of the kiln supported by a lintel that is formed by a single large stone or log, or in a few instances iron rails. The illustration shows sixteen basic designs found among Lancaster County lime kilns.

1. Brick arch, stone sides

2. Wide brick arch, stone sides

5. Entirely brick lined

6. Brick Gothic arch

9. Extended stone arch

10. Stone arch on short bases

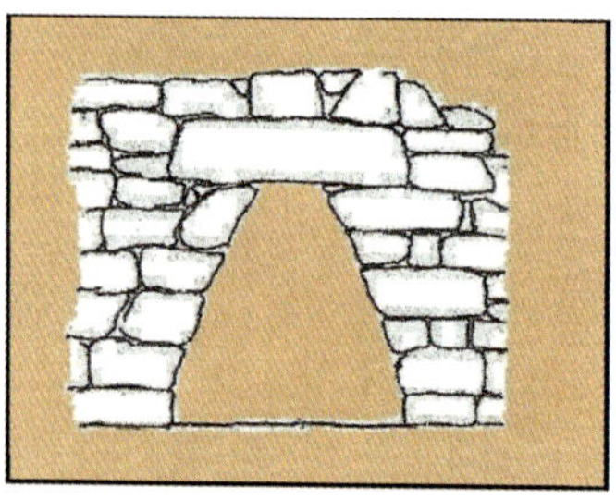

13. Truncated arch, heavy lintel

14. Vertical sides, massive stone lintel

3. Brick Roman arch, stone sides

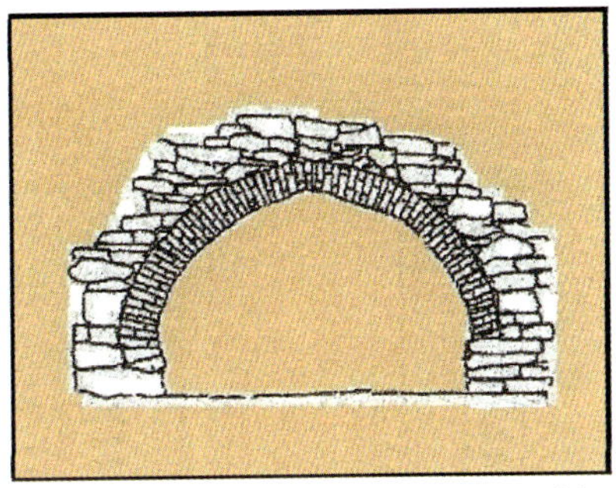

4. Brick Roman arch, short stone sides

7. Peaked brick arch

8. Stone arch, vertical sides

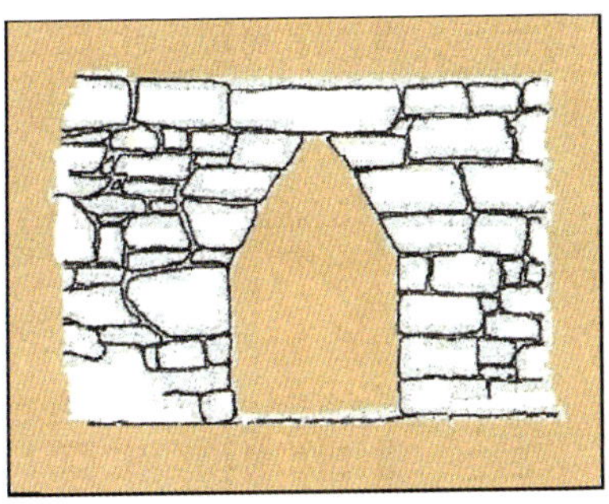

11. Corbelled stone arch

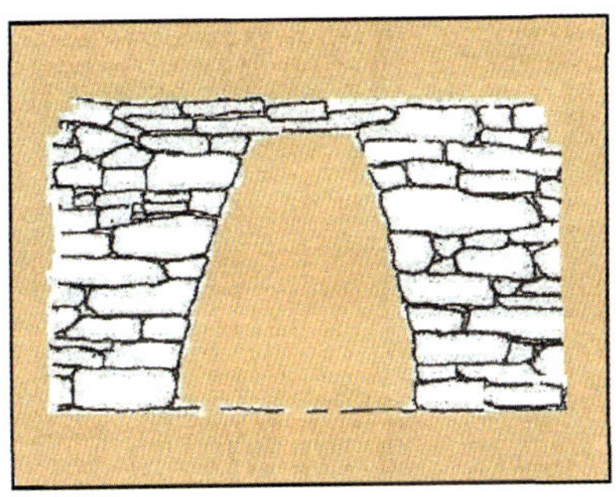

12. Truncated arch, thin stone lintel

15. Vertical sides, wooden lintel

16. Vertical sides, iron lintel

Diagrams of sixteen different designs appearing on the extant lime kilns in Lancaster County. *Drawn by the author*

SEVEN

A Catalog of Lancaster County Lime Kilns

"Ike Shirk's kiln across the Conestoga." *All photos in this section are by the author unless otherwise indicated*

No. 1: Shertzer's Meadow Lime Kiln

1

Shertzer's Meadow Lime Kiln (No. 1)

Spring blooming; wild columbines growing on the upper left corner of the kiln near a clump of purple cliffbrake ferns

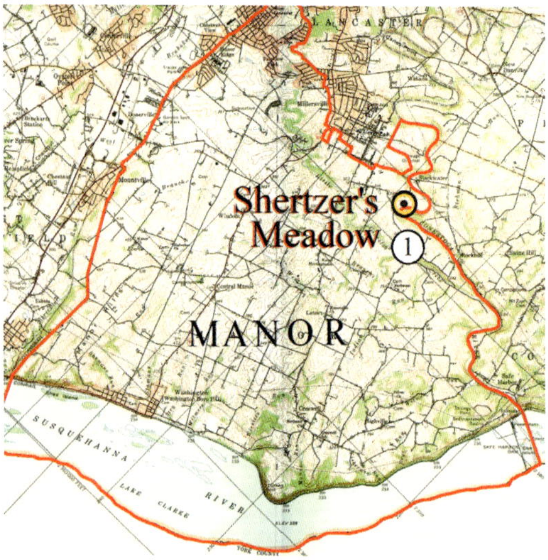

Manor Township. Topo. Kiln No. 1. N39.980144 W76.363716.

This secluded bucolic meadow, with the picturesque old lime kiln, faces the Conestoga River west of South Duke Street (Slackwater Road), a little more than a mile south of Millersville. Landis Shertzer bought the dairy farm in 1928, and it has now been in the family for three generations. The kiln came with the farm, and the current owner, his grandson Ken, doubts that his family ever burned it.

The "pot" is open at the top, and when Ken was asked if any cows had ever fallen in, he thought, "Maybe they had." How did they get them out? "Well, I guess they got themselves out," he chuckled. The arch looks large enough for a cow to get through, but the much-smaller draw hole at the back would seem to make the feat virtually analogous to the biblical phrase "a camel passing through the eye of a needle."

No. 2: Redbud Lime Kiln

2

Redbud Lime Kiln (No. 2)

Brown-colored ironstone rocks mixed in with the limestone, showing the dark interior of these fine-grained basaltic stones

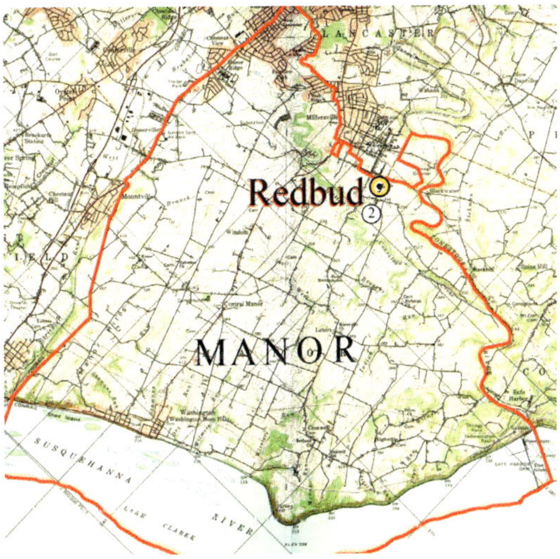

Manor Township. Topo. Kiln No. 2. N39.987961 W76.369782.

This lovely kiln of mostly local blue limestone is near Owl Bridge Road, 250 yards west of Sun Lane in Millersville Borough. It is similar in design to Shertzer's Meadow Kiln (No. 1), which is a bit more than half a mile to the south, suggesting it may have been built by the same mason.

The kiln is set into a narrow bank of erosion-resistant igneous rock that surfaces here and there as a ridge running north–south though Manor Township to the river. The close-up shows a handful of brown ironstone rocks included in the structure, which, when chipped or broken, reveal the typical dark, finely grained structure of these dibasic rocks.

No. 3: Charles Farm Lime Kiln

3

Implement shed atop the kiln, as seen from the rear

Manor Township. Topo. Kiln No. 3. N40.027694 W76.376092.

Charles Farm Lime Kiln (No. 3)

"Shed bearing" lime kilns sometimes show up in old photos, but they are seldom seen today. This especially tall one is hidden on a wooded hillside north of Charlestown Road in Manor Township, now owned by Armstrong World Industries.

It was purchased in 1960 from Abram B. Charles, after having been in the Charles family since 1774, when Jacob Charles purchased 40 acres from Henry Neff, then adding another 103 acres in 1791 from George Brenner.

The late Bishop Abram Charles, whose family operated the farm in the early 1930s, recalled helping his father cut logs to build a floor in the shed, which was open down into the kiln at that time. Thus the old structure, which was originally a covering for the burning kiln, was converted into a useful implement shed; one that is now abandoned (*see photo*).

No. 4: Prospect Road Gothic Lime Kiln

4

It is surprising to find a Gothic arch used in this otherwise rather rough lime kiln. The lower right side suggests that it may have originally been very nicely built. Repairs were made with less care. This sad-looking old kiln is hidden in a rocky copse in a field southwest of the intersection of Blue Rock Road and Prospect Road, just more than a mile east of Washington Borough.

One of two Gothic arches known in the county (the other being on Kinderhook Road, No. 41), it appears quite unstable and soon about to collapse.

At the top, red clay—typically used between the walls as fill and insulation—may be seen washing down over the front stones. The schematic diagram shows how the space between the pot and the outside wall was filled with red clay and debris, allowing the temperature inside the kiln to be maintained at approximately 1600°F for the limestone to be transformed into quicklime.

Prospect Road Gothic Lime Kiln (No. 4)

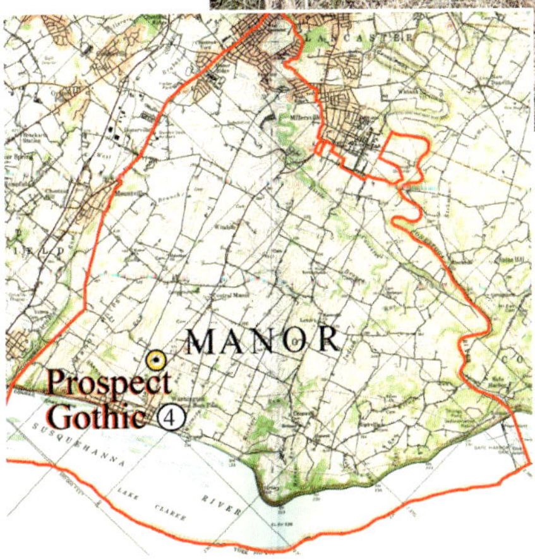

Manor Township. Topo. Kiln No. 4. N39.992661 W76.448031.

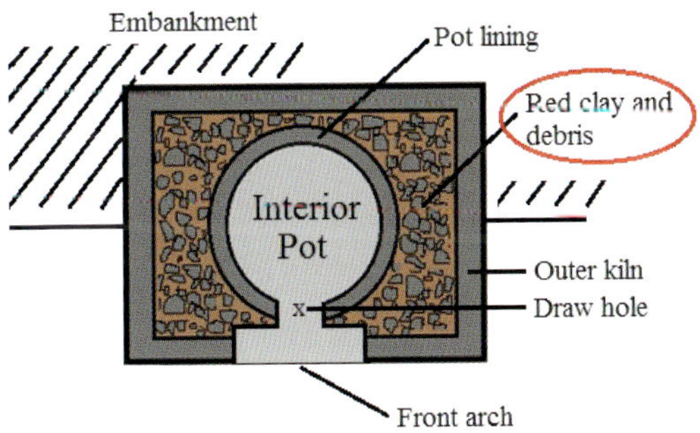

A schematic view from above, showing how the space between the outer and inner walls is filled with red clay and debris

No. 5: Conestoga House Lime Kiln

5

Conestoga House Lime Kiln (No. 5)

This architectural masterpiece is on the grounds of the Conestoga House and Gardens, just west of Lancaster City, where Marietta Pike crosses over Little Conestoga Creek.

The J. Hale Steinman estate, once an early-nineteenth-century farmstead, was purchased in 1927 and magnificently transformed into a jewel in the crown of Lancaster's most favorite places. The 1930s snapshot of the farm shows the old kiln with a frame shed that was replaced with the elegant pavilion (*left*).

Pavilion atop the kiln, as viewed from above

Snapshot of the old farm and kiln, ca. 1930

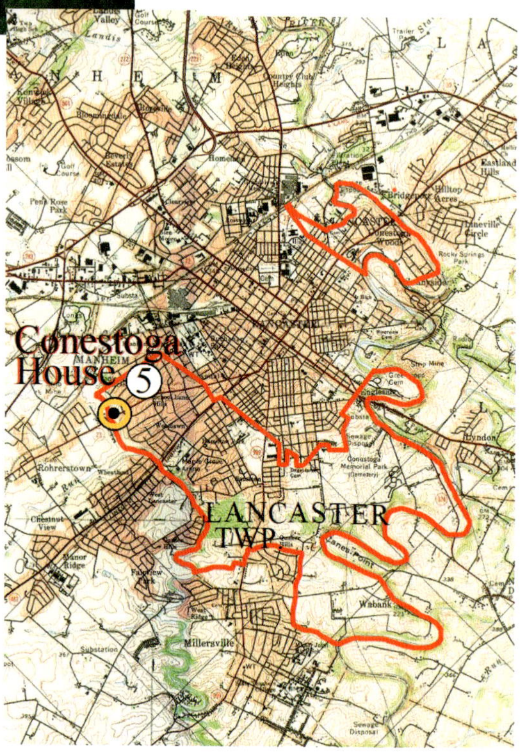

Lancaster Township. Topo. Kiln No. 5. N40.049053 W76.342044.

No. 6: Jacob Shenk's Lime Kiln

Jacob Shenk's Lime Kiln (No. 6)

A small container of Shenk's cup cheese ready to be served

This classic old lime kiln has weathered the years in excellent condition high above the banks of the Conestoga River along Route 324, three-quarters of a mile north of the small community of New Danville. When not hidden by the leaves, it may be seen to the south from the bridge over the river.

Like nearly all old kilns, we have no information on its early years, but it shares the distinction of being on the birthplace of Shenk's Cup Cheese, a local Pennsylvania Dutch favorite. A soft, spreadable cheese descendent of German *kochkase*, its flavor is said to be reminiscent of a strong brie.

The farm was purchased in 1892 by Jacob Shenk, and in 1929 his son, Clayton, began making cup cheese, which he sold at the downtown Lancaster Central Market. The business passed through several Shenk generations and is now produced by Shenk's Foods, Inc., on the old homestead not far from the old kiln.

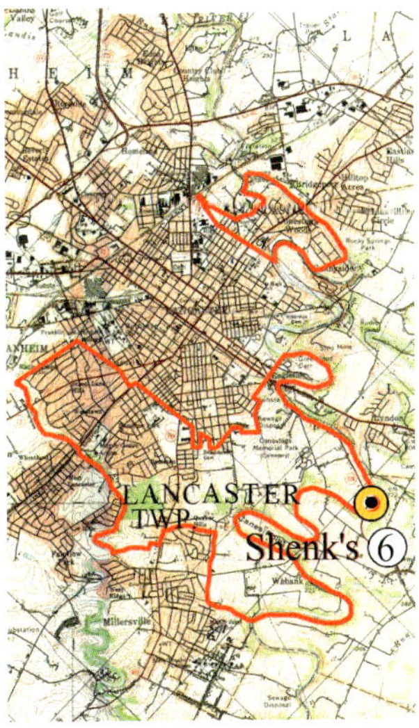

Lancaster Township. Topo. Kiln No. 6. N39.997156 W76.309799.

No. 7: Brenneman's Lime Kiln

Brenneman's Lime Kiln (No. 7)

This quaint old kiln is tucked away on a wooded hillside overlooking the Conestoga River, three-fourths of a mile north of New Danville.

It is dug into the bank in front of a large abandoned quarry. A second, adjacent quarry suggests that this was once a fair-sized quarrying and lime-burning operation. The two Brenneman brothers, who have recently turned the farm over to the next generation, know nothing about that business. It was long gone when their family bought the farm.

This is a favorite site for maidenhair spleenwort ferns, some of which are growing on the kiln, with many others on the nearby limestone outcrops.

The Brenneman family has raised produce on the farm for many years and operates the very popular "Corn Wagon" along Route 741 north of New Danville.

Pequea Township. Topo. Kiln No. 7. N39.995851 W76.309611.

Maidenhair spleenwort fern growing in the cracks of the kiln

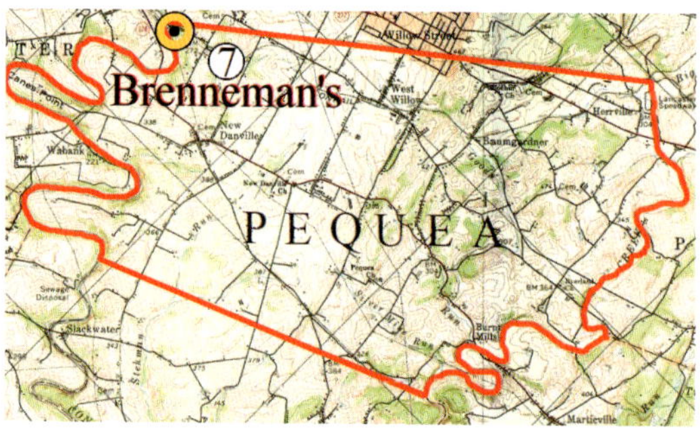

No. 8: Shultz Road Lime Kiln

8

This old lime kiln sits against a bank about 50 yards north of Shultz Road, a short distance west of Millwood Road. It may have been built by William L. Shultz, for whom the road was likely named, who purchased the property in 1909, or by Samuel Somerfield, who owned the farm before him.

During the early 1930s it was customary for itinerate hobos to hang out around these old, burned-out lime kilns. The Lancaster & Quarryville Railroad ran by less than a stone's throw from this kiln, where they could have easily hopped the train. Literature is replete with stories about these poor vagrants falling asleep by a kiln and being overcome by the fumes, to be found expired by the lime burners in the morning. The newspaper article is about a lime burner, rather than a hobo; nevertheless, it records a sad death at a lime kiln in Manor Township. These were dangerous places.

Shultz Road Lime Kiln (No. 8)

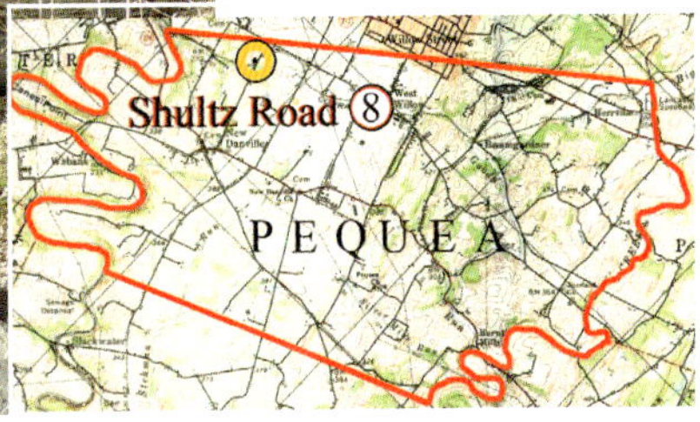

Pequea Township. Topo. Kiln No. 8. N39.990919 W76.295561.

"BURNED TO DEATH—At Masonville, Jacob Otto, aged about 45 years, lay down to sleep beside a lime kiln, which he had been burning for 25 years past, and while sleeping his clothes caught fire. He awoke to find himself enveloped in flames, and started on a rapid run for a stream of water about two hundred yards off, and [*sic*] on the bank of which he was found lying, with his clothing burned off, the flesh entirely stripped from one arm and his body burned almost to a crisp in some places. He was living when found, and was removed to the residence of Mr. Schupp nearby, where Dr. Davis was called and dressed his injuries. He lingered in great agony until Sunday morning, when death released him from his sufferings. The deceased leaves a wife and then children to mourn his untimely end. His funeral took place on Tuesday morning at 10 o'clock at Masonville"
(*Columbia Spy*, November 27, 1875).

No. 9: Myers Lime Kiln North

Myers Lime Kiln North (No. 9)

This neatly constructed blue-limestone kiln is 100 yards north of Long Lane (Route 741), one-half mile west of Millwood Road.

It is built of large, flat stones with clean, square box joint corners, the long side of the stone rotated 90 degrees every other course, nicely tying the walls together in the fashion of some log buildings. Many of the stones are exceptionally long, especially the top layer, with the one on the right measuring 9 feet. The wooden lintel of the arch—oak or chestnut—is itself 10 feet long. Although it has held things together for more than a hundred years, there is a slight sag noticeable, which probably accounts for the apparent loosening of the stones in the middle above it.

Box joint corners on (1) stone at Myers Lime Kiln North and (2) log house. Note the remnants of whitewash on the logs, which have been covered with siding for many years.

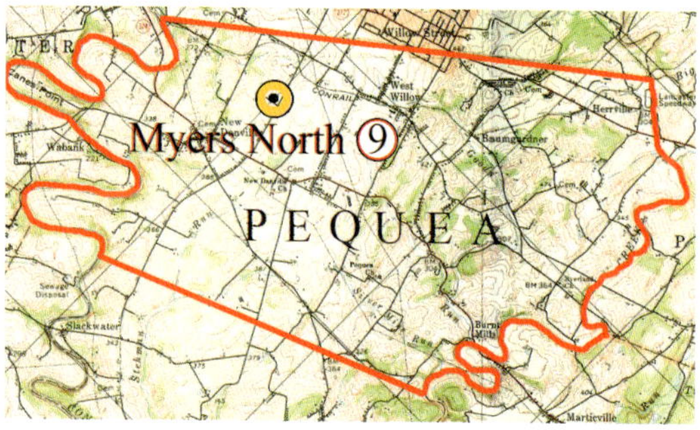

Pequea Township. Topo. Kiln No. 9. N39.982619 W76.295177.

No. 10: Myers Lime Kiln South

Myers Lime Kiln South (No. 10)

About 300 yards west of Millwood Road, along very heavily traveled Long Lane (Route 741) in Manor Township, we see this isolated old lime kiln in the middle of a desolate-looking field of corn stubble.

Although seen only when the corn is not in season, it is actually one of the more visible little lime kilns in the entire county, and one that is frequently called to the attention of this author.

Up close in the summertime, it is actually quite attractive, with its lovely little red-brick arch embedded in a wall of blue-gray limestone that is enshrouded in a cover of poison ivy and surrounded by various shades of green trees and brush.

A hundred or so years ago it would have been the scene of a hot, noisy, smoky, and dirty lime furnace—*kalik offe*, as the old Germans would have called it.

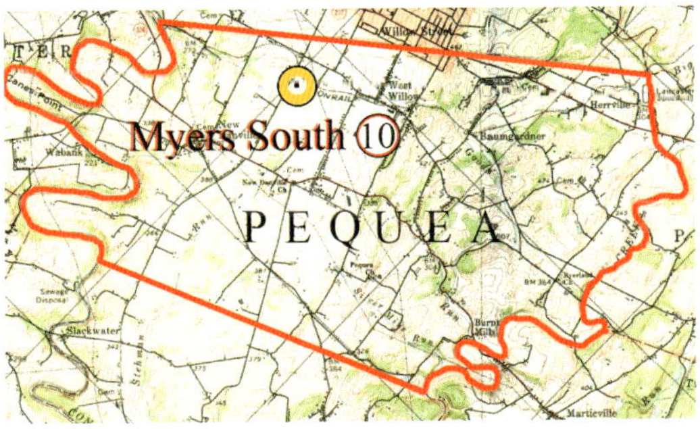

Pequea Township. Topo. Kiln No. 10. N39.982979 W76.295001.

Myers Lime Kiln in the middle of the field, looking south from Long Lane

No. 11: Shallowbrook Farm Lime Kiln

11

Shallowbrook Farm Lime Kiln (No. 11)

Strasburg Township. Topo. Kiln No. 11. N39.945708 W76.242669.

This rugged-looking kiln built of heavy limestone blocks stands on a secluded wooded hillside on a private farm 0.3 miles north of Smithville Road and is inaccessible except by permission.

Even though it appears to have been well built, the stones have loosened up. The massive stone lintel that once filled the space above the arch has become dislodged and now lies in front on the ground. Another huge limestone slab still remains in place and continues to do its job of holding up the heavy weight above it. The draw hole at the far end of the archway is fairly large and would have allowed entrance into the kiln to begin to build the base of the charge.

Looking into the deep archway at the heavy stone lintels, the front one having fallen to the ground

No. 12: Red Fox Lime Kiln

Red Fox Lime Kiln (No. 12)

These nice-looking blue-limestone ruins are southwest of Millersville on Owl Bridge Road, approximately a half mile south of Walnut Hill Road.

Although the central portion has collapsed, enough remains to show that the entrance was formed with a lintel rather than a rounded arch.

It is less than 50 feet from the road and behind a slight ridge, facing south, and cannot be seen without entering the property owner's private driveway. A computerized restoration (*right*) shows what the kiln may have looked like before its collapse.

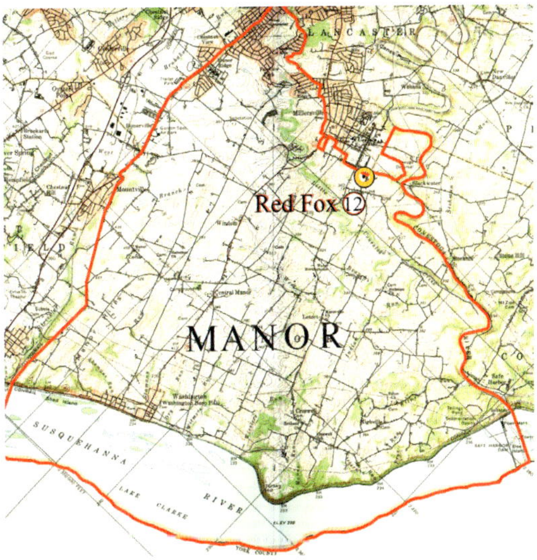

Manor Towuship. Topo. Kiln No. 12. N39.983960 W76.376764.

Computerized restoration showing how this kiln would likely have appeared before the front crumbled

Miniatures on the Walls of Red Fox Lime Kiln

Miniatures on the walls of Red Fox Lime Kiln
1. slag (melted rock), 2. coarse moss, 3. fungus spore capsules, 4. blunt-lobed woodsia fern, 5. foliose lichen, 6. fine moss with sporophytes, 7. black moss, 8. moss with large sporophytes, and 9. crustose lichen

The rocks of lime kilns provide excellent niches for small mosses, ferns, and lichens, especially in shaded areas. Here we see some examples growing on Red Fox Lime Kiln (No. 12).

No. 13: Pickle Farm Lime Kiln

Close-up of the "box" in the right wing

Pickle Farm Lime Kiln (No. 13)

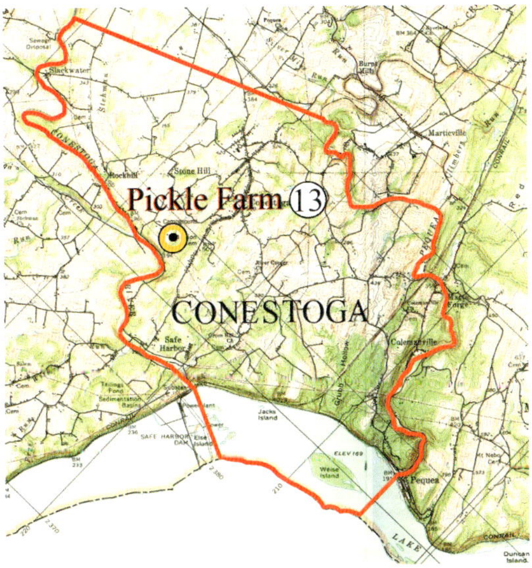

Conestoga Township. Topo. Kiln No. 13. N39.945206 W76.363286.

This unique kiln is hidden in the woods of Conestoga Township, 1.2 miles south of Rockhill. The trail from Conestoga Boulevard leads up along a brook through the Promised Land Camp property, 0.2 miles past the kiln.

The front of the kiln is uniquely constructed, with wings extending forward on either side at an angle from the arch. A small chamber is built into both wings. Such a box is sometimes found in other kilns, the purpose of which we may only speculate. Did it play some role in the operation of the kiln, or was it a place to store tools, food, drink, etc.?

An item of personal history relating to this kiln is that the author's maternal grandfather, William Gerlach, was a tenant on this farm in the early 1900s. It was then owned by a Dr. Pickle from Columbia. My mother would have been a young teen at the time, and I have visions of her and her siblings sneaking away in the woods to explore the old kiln, which was certainly no longer in use by that time.

No. 14: Stone Hill Road Lime Kiln

14

Stone Hill Road Lime Kiln (No. 14)

This handsome, well-cared-for kiln faces Stone Hill Road, 0.7 miles west of Conestoga in Conestoga Township. It is solidly constructed of schist, the principal underlying rock of southern Lancaster County.

The owner related how they purchased the property not realizing they were buying a lime kiln, which was then hidden in the brush. Now they illuminate it with floodlights and proudly adorn it from time to time with conservative decorations such as a wreath. Note also the owner's house entrance (*below left*) with the "kiln-matching" arch.

Front entrance to the owner's house (out of sight behind the kiln), resembling the lime kiln arch.

Conestoga Township. Topo. Kiln No. 14. N39.948273 W76.345456.

No. 15: Spring Run Lime Kiln

15

Spring Run Lime Kiln (No. 15)

Receding into the lush forest landscape like a Frank Lloyd Wright masterpiece, this quaint kiln is hidden in the woodlands near Safe Harbor in Conestoga Township. It is about 100 yards west along the Spring Run trail, which enters the woods from Spring Run Road 0.3 miles north of River Road and 1.5 miles east of Safe Harbor.

The rectangular arch supports a 9-foot weathered log lintel. It is remarkable how these wooden—oak and hickory—lintels have held up for well more than 100 years.

The kiln was most certainly built before the Safe Harbor Water Power Company purchased the property in 1900, but it is not in the 1875 atlas, making its construction sometime during the last quarter of the nineteenth century. We have no other information regarding its ownership or operation.

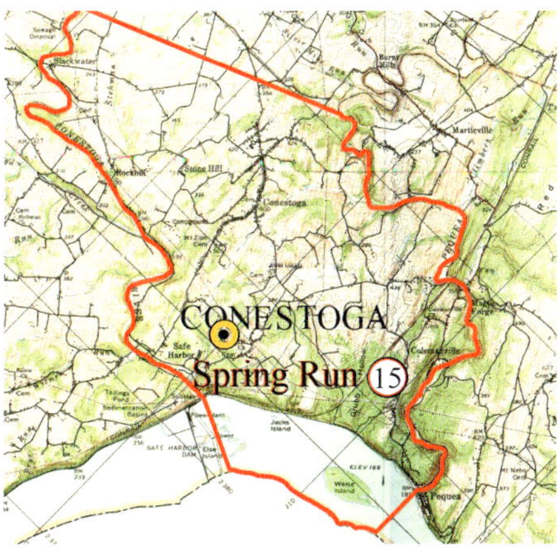

Conestoga Township. Topo. Kiln No. 15. N39.928944 W76.370602.

Blunt-lobed woodsia fern growing in the joints of the front wall

No. 16: Nissley's Vineyard Lime Kiln

16

Nissley's Vineyard Lime Kiln (No. 16)

This sturdy, attractive lime kiln is built into the bank immediately behind the attractive winery building at Nissley's Vineyard.

The structure was wonderfully restored by Mr. Richard Nissley, who was a bridge-building engineer before "retiring" to the winery business in 1978. It is still operated by the Nissley family today.

The top of the kiln is graced by an old iron railing that Mr. Nissley salvaged when the old Landisville Hotel was demolished. He also built, or rebuilt, the lovely stone bridge nearby over Conoy Creek, several hundred yards from the winery and the lime kiln above.

The winery at Nissley's Vineyard. The kiln is off the picture to the right.

Four-arch bridge over Conoy Creek on the vineyard grounds

Conoy Township. Topo. Kiln No. 16. N40.089507 W76.646983.

Nos. 17 and 18: James Logan Lime Kilns

James Logan Lime Kilns (Nos. 17 and 18)

This stately set of lime kilns is built into the hillside facing west over the Little Conestoga Creek and South Creek Drive, one-quarter mile north of the confluence of Little Conestoga Creek with the Conestoga River.

Double kilns like this would have been burned alternately, one being emptied of lime while the other was loaded with limestone. In the early eighteenth century the land across the creek was part of "Penn's Manor," with the office of James Logan, his land agent, several hundred yards downstream from where these kilns now stand.

The kiln is currently on the property of Robert Hershey but was in the Lefever family from the early 1800s until 1951. Presumably they would have operated these kilns. The right arch is supported by a small but definite keystone not often seen in kiln arches.

Top of the arch of Kiln No. 17, showing the small keystone

Manor Township. Topo. Kiln Nos. 17 and 18. N39.954398 W76.369864.

19

No. 19: Martin Barr Farm Lime Kiln

The Martin Barr Farm Lime Kiln (No. 19)

Wild columbines growing in front of the lime kiln

The historic Martin Barr house in 2015

Strasburg Township. Topo. Kiln No. 19. N39.946895 W76.217958.

This interesting lime kiln is on the historic "Martin Barr Farm" in Strasburg Township, 445 Walnut Run Road, northeast of the intersection of Beaver Valley Pike (Route 222) and Walnut Run Road.

The farm is listed on the National Register of Historic Places; its nomination form mentions the existence of a lime kiln in 1994. The kiln is set into the rocky hillside, with 6-foot "wings" angled forward at about 30 degrees from the front of the same width. The heavy brick Roman arch, missing the facing bricks, sits atop stone sidewalls, with the chamber leading back about 2 feet to a heavy stone "wall," within which is a 20-inch-wide draw hole.

To the lower left of the arch is an interesting small "box" roughly 12 inches square, built into the wall and formed with worked sandstone blocks, about 10 inches deep and closed at the back, similar to those found on the Pickle Farm Lime Kiln (No. 13).

The kiln, depicted in the 1875 but not the 1864 atlas, may have been built by Henry Leaman, who owned the property in that period. The house on this historic farmstead is said to have been built between 1741 and 1791, likely evolving from a single-story stone house into its current structure. Though it's known as the "Martin Barr House," Leaman in fact purchased it from Jacob Haines Barr in 1764. Martin was a Mennonite farmer, miller, and landowner in Strasburg, according to *The Historic Preservation Trust of Lancaster County*.

Nos. 20a and 20b: Peoples's Hatchery Lime Kilns

Peoples's Hatchery Lime Kilns (Nos. 20a and 20b)

This set of lime kilns is dug into the bank along a private driveway at the southern end of the village of New Providence. Entering town from the south on Main Street, they can be seen on the left from the bridge crossing a small stream.

We call them Peoples's Hatchery Lime Kilns because the property was once owned by the Honorable Hiram Peoples, a prominent civic leader, farmer, entrepreneur, and longtime member of the Pennsylvania House of Representatives. Mr. Peoples was born in 1835 and grew up on this 90-acre farm of his father. He must have built these kilns shortly after 1864, since they appear only in the 1875 atlas.

In 1880 he began experimenting with raising fish; first carp, bass, and other warm-water fish before switching to goldfish and developing what was once recognized as the largest hatchery in the state. The operation was eventually taken over by Henry Stagers, who grew the business and by 1972, according to an article in *Lancaster Farming* magazine, was raising and selling three and a half million goldfish per year.

Old ponds of the fish hatchery

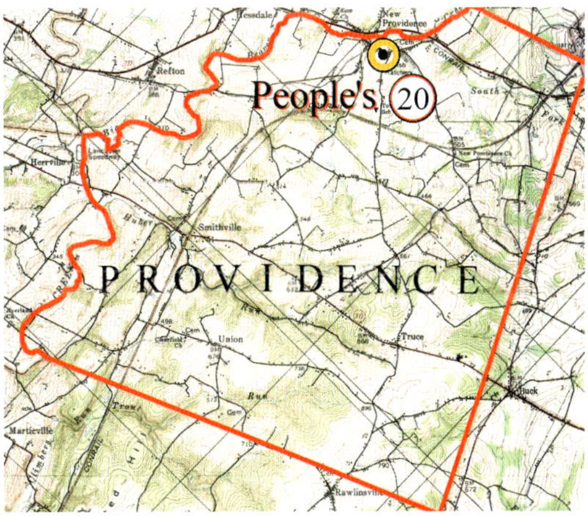

Providence Township. Topo. Kiln No. 20. N39.921856 W76.195822

No. 21: Camargo East Lime Kiln

Camargo East Lime Kiln (No. 21)

This solid-looking lime kiln remains perched atop the hill overlooking Big Beaver Creek, meandering through the "Camargo Valley," one-quarter mile east of Route 222.

The apparently well-built archway belies the fact that so little of the kiln front remains, suggesting that the large cut stones were deliberately removed to be used for another purpose elsewhere. The relatively tall, narrow, truncated arch did not require as massive a lintel as we often see on wider arches with straight sides. This great variety of structure and design is one of the fascinating aspects of this study.

Big Beaver Creek meanders through the meadow below the kiln.

Strasburg Township. Topo. Kiln No. 21. N39.920281 W76.182886.

No. 22: Archery Road Lime Kiln

22

This picturesque and ancient-looking lime kiln emerges from the hillside on the grounds of a former plantation along Archery Road, approximately 2 miles northwest of Quarryville.

Resembling the previous kiln, Camargo East (No. 21), although built with smaller stones, it is characterized by the same tall, truncated archway with a wide, thin draw hole capped by a large stone lintel.

Remains of two other kilns were within 100 yards of this kiln but have since been demolished during a landscaping project.

Archery Road Lime Kiln (No. 22)

Ice-covered walls in a quarry behind the kiln

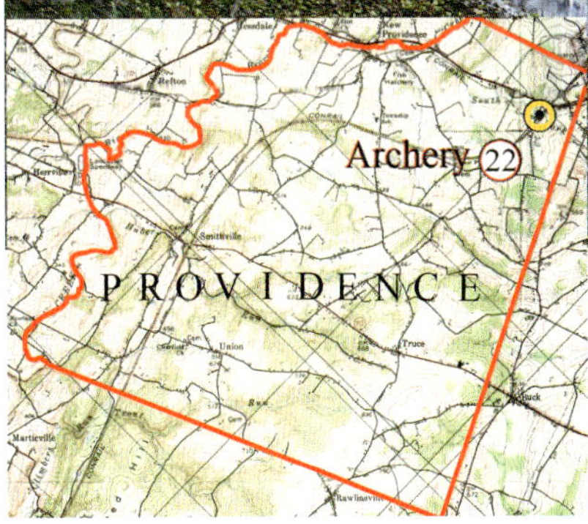

Providence Township. Topo. Kiln No. 22. N39.903750 W76.184901.

No. 23: Penn Grant Road Lime Kiln

23

Penn Grant Road Lime Kiln (No. 23)

Looking down into the burning chamber or pot of the Penn Grant Road kiln.

This charming, well-kept blue-limestone kiln is in the front lawn of a home on Penn Grant Road, 2.5 miles west of Strasburg.

The solid log lintel over the arch has weathered the seasons in excellent condition. Not only is the exterior well built and maintained, but the same may be said for the interior pot (*left*). The touch of an English ivy mantle and the yellow forsythia adds to its attractiveness.

This property was once part of a much-larger farm purchased by an Amish farmer half a century ago. Now he is retired to his *grussdaudy* (attached grandparent's dwelling) on his farm nearby, and the author approached him to learn something about the kiln. He thought for a moment, "Well, ah . . . chust came with the farm," and smiled. Of course, it had not felt the heat of burning lime for at least another half century before he bought it.

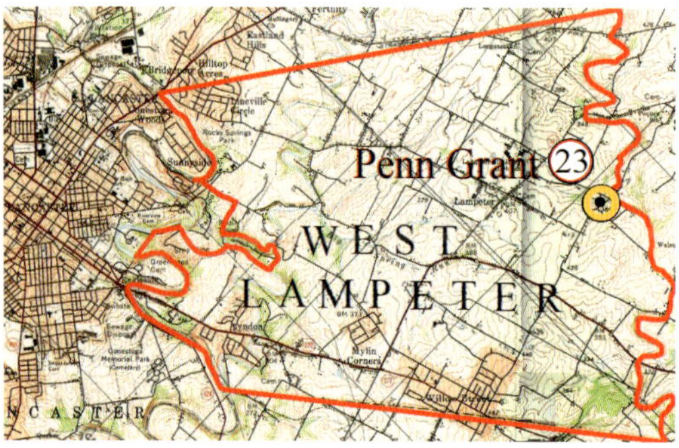

West Lampeter Township. Topo. Kiln No. 23. N39.979268 W76.228334.

No. 24: Rineer's Lime Kiln

Rineer's Lime Kiln (No. 24)

At the end of a private driveway west off Strasburg Pike, approximately a mile north of Strasburg, we find this interesting kiln that has been modified for a second life. The water source for the house nearby is uphill and piped into the archway of the kiln, which has been reinforced with brick and wooden doors to enclose the pump and storage tank.

Although it would have been constructed nearly two hundred years after the first Pequea Mennonite settlement, it is located within the 1,060-acre tract granted to Martin Kundig in 1710. A plaque memorializing the settlement stands in front of the Willow Street Mennonite Church on Penn Grant Road (*see photo*). The location of the Rineer kiln is marked on the photo with a red dot.

The following page shows the kiln location on an enlargement of the Pequea settlement, superimposed on topographic maps of the three townships involved (Pequea, Strasburg, and West Lampeter) and locating the kiln sites for 1864, 1875, and 2015.

Strasburg Township. Topo. Kiln No. 24. N39.991853 W76.203027.

A plaque on the grounds of the Willow Street Mennonite Church commemorating the 1710 Pequea Mennonite settlement

Original Tracts of 1710 Pequea Settlement

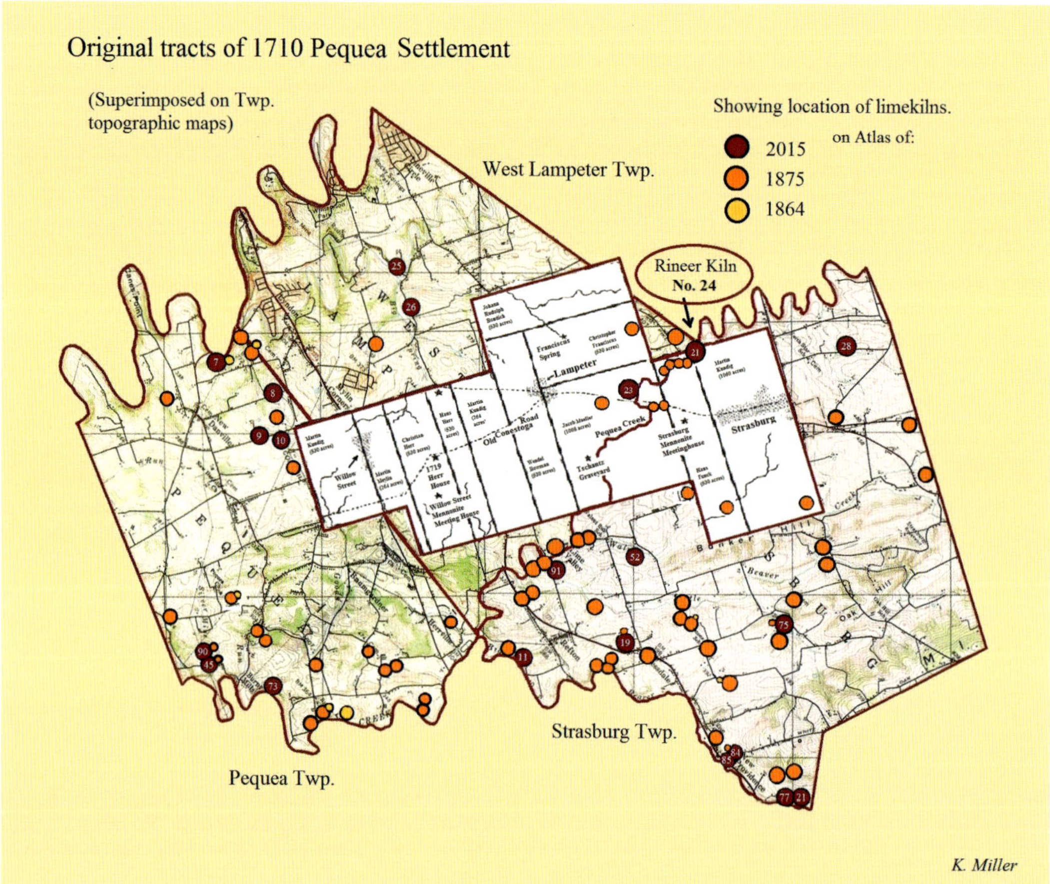

Topographic maps of Pequea, Strasburg, and West Lampeter Townships overlain with a draft of the original tracts in the 1710 settlement, along with the locations of lime kilns from the current project (2019) and the 1864 and 1875 atlas maps.

No. 25: Gypsy Hill Road North Lime Kiln

Gypsy Hill Road North Lime Kiln (No. 25)

This small lime kiln was built just off the roadside along Gypsy Hill Road, approximately 0.2 miles north of the bridge crossing over Mill Creek.

It is fairly nondescript, built of limestone rocks of all shapes and sizes. The singular unique feature would be the flat poured-concrete lintel—the only example known to be standing today. The top and rear inside the archway are constructed with three large limestone rocks that are stepped downward to the draw hole, which is nearly obscured with soil and debris.

The poured-concrete lintel above the arch

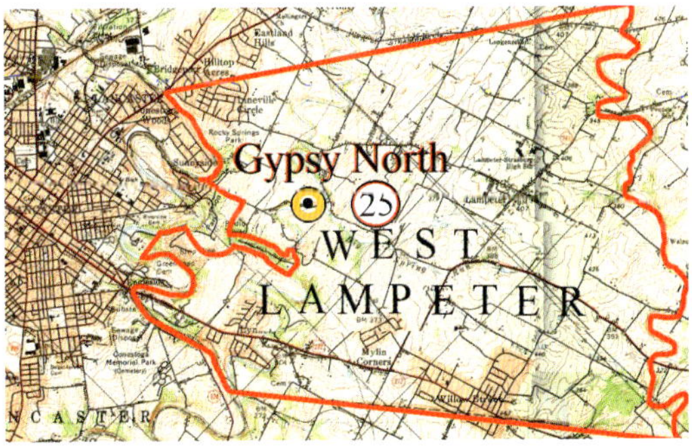

West Lampeter Township. Topo. Kiln No. 25. N40.011715 W72.270245.

Nos. 26a and 26b: Gypsy Hill Road South Lime Kilns

26

Gypsy Hill Road South Lime Kilns (Nos. 26a and 26b)

Left draw arch, Kiln No. 26a

Right draw arch, Kiln No. 26b

This crisp-looking set of lime kilns may be the "most noticed" in the county. They are built at a highly visible location, literally on the edge of heavily traveled Gypsy Hill Road, a mile north of Beaver Valley Pike (Route 222). One must take a brief, quick look in driving by, since the road is narrow, near the crest of a hill with no place to slow down or stop.

The neatly built blue-limestone kiln's twin arches are nearly a perfect match, even to the identical crack in the lower lintel of the draw hole. In the summertime the kilns are heavily shrouded in a lush growth of poison ivy.

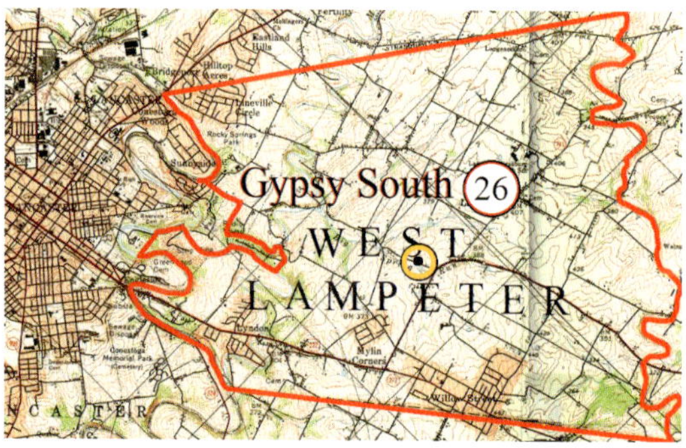

West Lampeter Township. Topo. Kiln Nos. 26a and 26b. N40.004834 W76.266313.

No. 27: Young's Lane Lime Kiln

27

"Box" in the right wing of the archway

Young's Lane Lime Kiln (No. 27)

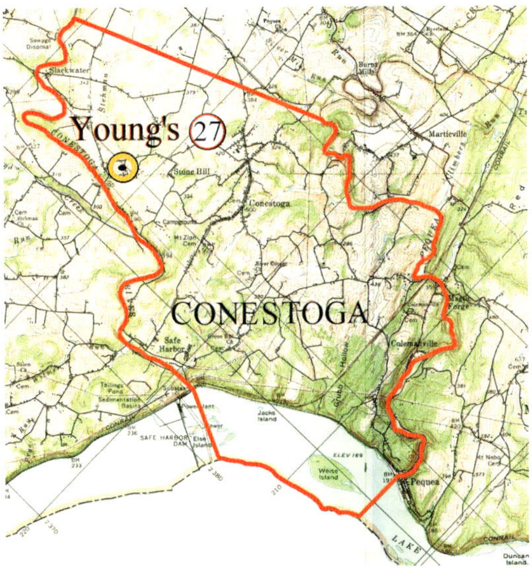

Conestoga Township. Topo. Kiln No. 27. N39.960960 W76.358314.

This ancient-looking kiln on the wooded hillside along a farm lane off Stone Hill Road in Pequea Township might well be considered ruins. We include it here because there is something attractive in its relatively stabilized "eye" peering out from the hillside.

Evidence would suggest that the stones of the front wall were removed long ago to be used in building a bridge or wall. The roof of the archway is constructed of tightly fitting bricks, with a heavy iron bar supporting several huge stones in the draw hole inside.

It is interesting to note the small box hole on the right, several feet from the very front of the archway. Similar holes, whose purpose remains a mystery, are found in the Pickle Farm Lime Kiln (No. 13) and a few other kilns around the county.

No. 28: North Star Road Lime Kiln

28

North Star Road Lime Kiln (No. 28)

This especially long kiln stands out boldly on the hillside about 170 yards north of North Star Road, north of Strasburg.

It is constructed entirely of nicely laid blue limestone. The left end appears to have been rebuilt or reinforced. An unusually large limestone slab is used as a lintel. Little else can be mentioned regarding the kiln, other than a personal note.

Levi, a friend of the author, tells how as a young Amish man growing up on a neighboring farm, he was occasionally sent over to work the fields near the kiln, which his father owned. He recalls how, on at least one occasion, he crawled into the arch as a place of refuge during a heavy thunderstorm. Presumably his team withstood the elements outside.

Strasburg Township. Topo. Kiln No. 28. N39.996301 W76.167099.

A young Amish farmer working the fields with his eight-mule team

No. 29: Cherry Crest Farm Lime Kiln

29

Cherry Crest Farm Lime Kiln (No. 29)

In a quiet meadow along Cherry Hill Road, 2.75 miles east of Strasburg, we find this architecturally fascinating lime kiln. The arch itself is not necessarily unusual, but the draw hole is a charming truncated triangle reminiscent of an Egyptian motif. Only one other kiln of like design is in the county, roughly 8 miles east, near Millwood Road in Salisbury Township (Kiln No. 30).

The modern dairy buildings in the background present a contrasting image against this agricultural relic of our past.

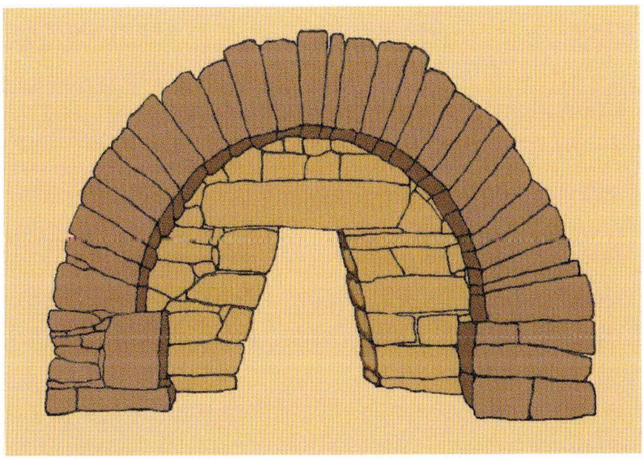

Diagram of the arch and draw hole, suggestive of an Egyptian motif

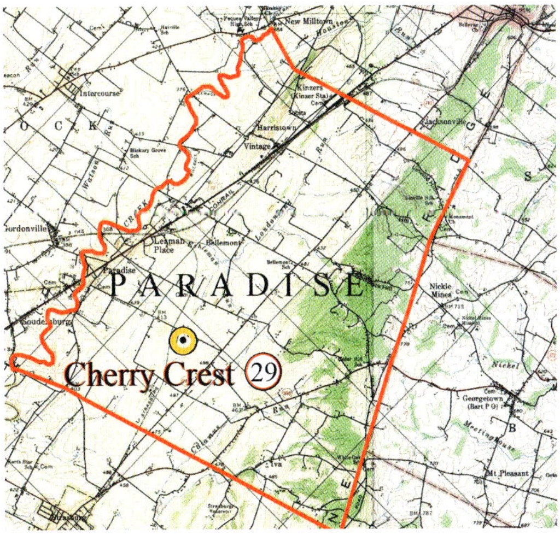

Paradise Township. Topo. Kiln No. 29. N39.989894 W76.129570.

No. 30: Millwood Road Lime Kiln

30

Millwood Road Lime Kiln (No. 30)

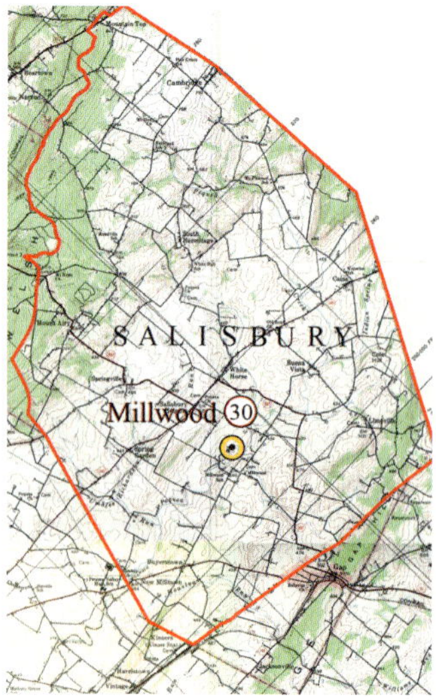

Salisbury Township. Topo. Kiln No. 30. N40.022002 W76.011366.

Millwood Road Lime Kiln (*left*) and Cherry Crest Lime Kiln (*right*)

In a hidden meadow behind farm buildings, 0.3 miles from Millwood Road, this interesting lime kiln watches over Pequea Creek approximately 100 yards to its south.

With its Egyptian-looking draw hole peering out through the lovely Roman arch, this kiln looks virtually identical to the ruins on Cherry Crest Farm (Kiln No. 29), 3 miles east of Strasburg. Although nearly 7 miles apart, these two kilns are so unique and so similar that one can't help but wonder if there was a connection between their builders.

The Millwood kiln in the trees, overlooking a lush meadow and meandering Pequea Creek in eastern Lancaster County

No. 31: Snake Lane Lime Kiln

Snake Lane Lime Kiln (No. 31)

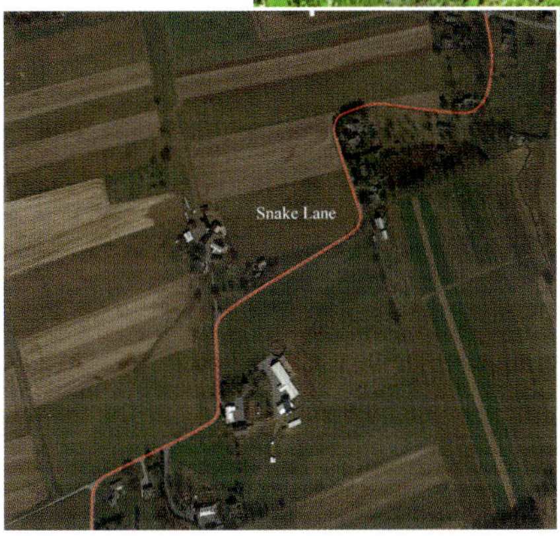

The line marks Snake Lane following the old boundary lines through Salisbury Township, described on a Google Earth map.

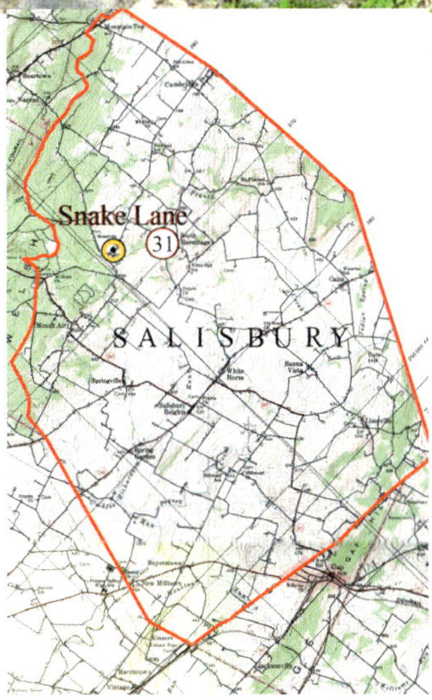

Salisbury Township. Topo. Kiln No. 31. N40.053343 W76.030154.

This old kiln, rudely built of an assortment of fieldstones, stands in a pasture beside a small quarry 300 yards north of Peters Road and 140 yards west of Snake Lane.

Although crumbling mortar remains in the joints, both top corners have fallen away and approximately half of the small pot—roughly 8 feet in diameter—has fallen in. The remaining portion is heavily coated with slag.

Although there is no arch visible, a huge, 6-foot-long stone overlies the small front opening, nearly hidden by a large mound of soil excavated by some unknown varmints, likely groundhogs. The 18-inch-square draw hole extends directly from the front face to the pot inside.

We may wonder about the name "Snake Lane," but an aerial view from Google Earth showing a winding mile-long section from Route 340 to Peters Road offers strong evidence for the origin of the name.

No. 32: Hartman Patent Lime Kiln

Hartman Patent Lime Kiln (No. 32)

Out of sight from surrounding roads, this unusual lime kiln stands in an open pasture less than half a mile north of Conestoga Valley High School.

It is a freestanding commercial kiln, unlike other farm kilns in the county, which are typically built into a bank or hillside. This would have required some system for getting limestone to the top, such as a long ramp or a winch and pulley, both of which were in use at the time. The offset in the upper left corner and the concrete slab at the top no doubt played a role, but there is no indication of just how this task was done, and no pictures or descriptions have as yet been located.

The design is that of a patent kiln with continuous operation, with the lime removed day and night while the limestone was added from above. At the same time, fuel was fed into a fire chamber from the side opening into the pot, heating the stone to the temperature at which it would turn into lime.

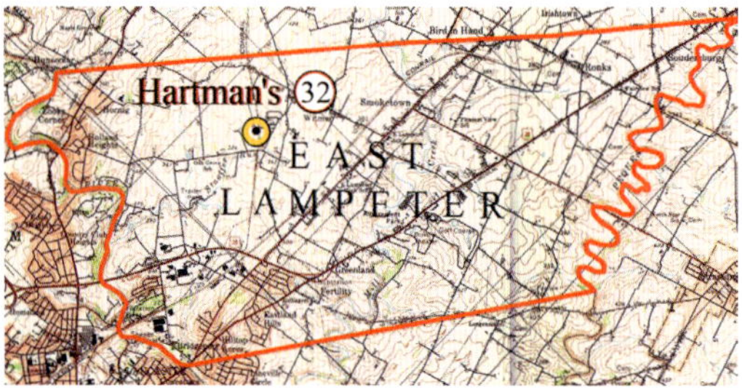

East Lampeter Township. Topo. Kiln No. 32. N40.055618 W76.226747.

A drawing from the original patent. *Patent Office archives*

The operation is more fully explained, along with a brief history of the Hartman Lime Kiln business, below. (Note: The site has limited access, and permission should be obtained before visiting the kiln.)

The Hartman Patent Lime kiln may have looked something like this schematic based on other examples in the literature, including the old photograph of the Elias Herr Kiln operating approximately the same time near Refton, in Lancaster County.

The kiln has an interesting and uncertain history. Evidence suggests that it was built and operated by Henry K. Hartman. Born in Bavaria on January 20, 1831, Mr. Hartman immigrated to America and eventually settled in East Lampeter Township, where, in 1872, he purchased 25 acres of land from the James Landis estate, near what is now Hartman's Station.

The deed included mention of a lime kiln on the property, and Hartman developed a very successful lime-burning business, eventually adding another 15 acres and additional kilns. He died on June 27, 1899, and his estate was sold at auction in 1900. The property remained in the family, and we read in the *Biographical Annals of Lancaster County* (Meginness 1903) that his son David "now operates the old lime kilns of his father." Presumably that included Kiln No. 32.

We cannot establish for certain that Henry K. actually built these kilns, but there are records in the US patent archives that establish that "a Hartman" (first name absent), on September 3, 1871, purchased the rights to "build and use" a "patented kiln" in East Lampeter Township.

View of the kiln from the railroad tracks

A drawing attached to the original patent of 1861 superficially resembles Kiln No. 32.

Although his son David was also in the lime business, he was not born until 1866 and would have been just five years old at the time of the patent purchase; thus he was not the unnamed Hartman on that deed, nor was his brother John K., who was also in the lime business. John was born in 1873, twelve years after the patent purchase. There were other Hartmans in East Lampeter Township at the time, but none ever owned the tract where this kiln was built, so it is somewhat of a mystery; although we cannot say for certain that it was built by Henry K., the evidence suggests that he likely did.

The site was owned by Landis families throughout the nineteenth century, from the time that Henry Landis purchased 71 acres from John Kurtz in 1796. It is a good example of how difficult it is to track down the origin and history of these kilns.

Elias Herr Lime Kiln near Refton, Pennsylvania, operating approximately the same period as Hartman Patent Lime Kiln. We know the site of the Herr kiln, but there is not a shred of evidence to be found.

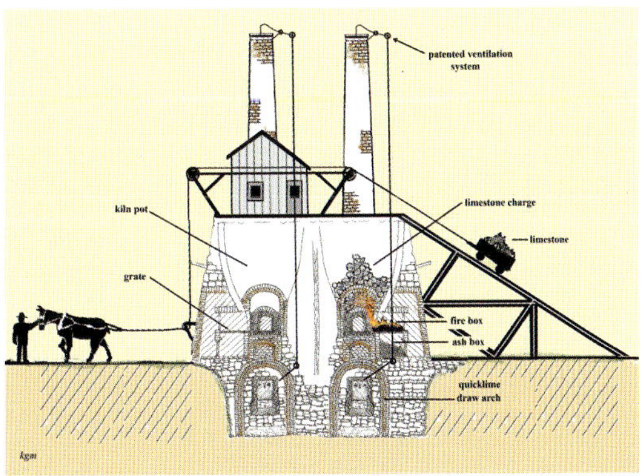

A theoretical schematic of Hartman kiln as it may have looked during operation. *Author*

No. 33: Voganville Road Lime Kiln

33

Voganville Road Lime Kiln (No. 33)

This sturdy-looking kiln constructed of a solid, light-colored limestone dug into a limestone outcrop is visible across the meadow from Voganville Road, just west of New Holland.

Its survival is severely threatened by the two large, wild black cherry trees entrenched in its upper walls, though it is somewhat strengthened by the two wings constructed outward on either side.

To the left there is evidence of at least one, probably two, additional kilns, although there is little left of them except piles of stones. Apparently it was once a thriving lime-burning operation, with the lime being carted up to the railroad along Route 23, bound for Philadelphia markets.

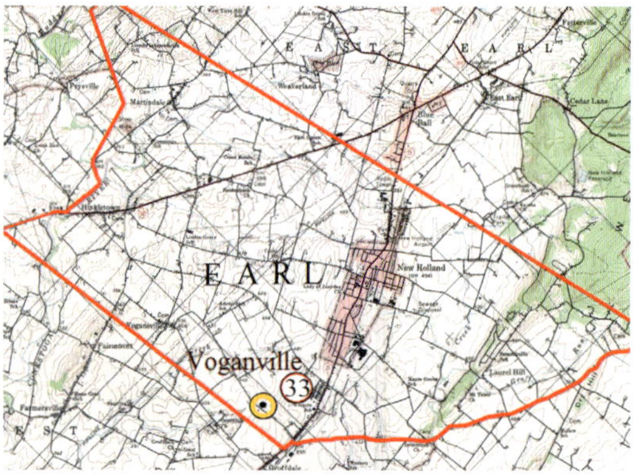

Earl Township. Topo. Kiln No. 33. N40.096207 W76.124164.

Voganville Road kiln in the bank across the meadow

Nos. 34a and 34b: Poole Forge Lime Kilns

Poole Forge Lime Kilns (Nos. 34a and 34b)

This attractive set of double kilns is dug into the bank on the west side of the Conestoga River, facing the Iron Masters Mansion at Poole Forge along Route 23, approximately three-quarters of a mile west of the village of Churchtown.

The kilns were built of a colorful mixture of sandstone and limestone, apparently at different times. Although they fit snugly together, there is a clear demarcation where the two kilns join. The arches are also slightly different, with the left one being larger and taller.

The arches open directly into the pot, without the smaller draw hole that is found on many kilns. This would have necessitated placing iron bars across the inside when the kiln was loaded. Bars for this purpose were found in the debris when the kiln was restored, and are now stored in one of the buildings on the grounds.

Historic Poole Forge is a beautifully restored iron plantation with elements dating to the late 1700s. The park features the iron master's mansion, paymaster's house, tenant houses, lime kilns, and the 1859 vintage covered bridge passing over the Conestoga River.

A covered bridge over the Conestoga River near the kilns on the Poole Forge grounds

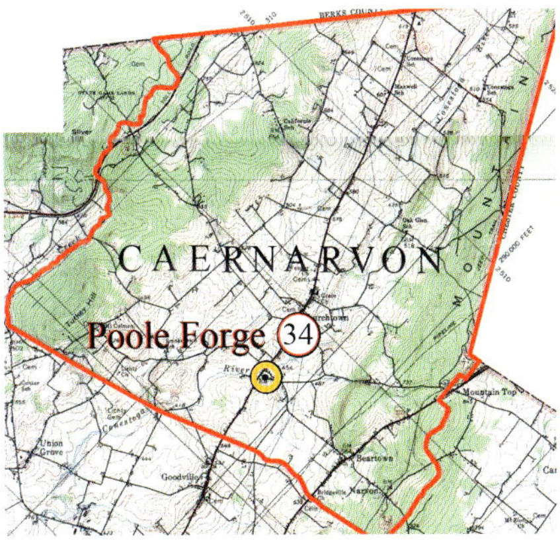

Caernarvon Township. Topo. Kiln Nos. 34a and 34b. N40.132742 W75.950042.

No. 35: Ike Shirk's Lime Kiln

35

Ike Shirk's Lime Kiln (No. 35)

This sturdy sandstone relic we believe might be the oldest extant lime kiln in Lancaster County, on the basis of its design.

Lime kilns were surely built here by the first settlers in the early 1700s, but we have no evidence or records of specific kilns earlier than this one. It is south of Route 23, just east of Churchtown, resting on the banks of the Conestoga River, where it is still a shallow stream meandering through the meadows of Caernarvon Township.

Some years ago, when Mr. Shirk had it cleaned out and stabilized, a set of stone ledges were discovered, forming a central trench from the front arch to the back of the kiln (*see diagram*). Undoubtedly, a series of iron bars were laid across the shelves to support the limestone charge while the fire was maintained in the trench below, and from which the quicklime was recovered. This unique feature has not been found on other kilns in the county. An article in the *Village Record* from March 27, 1822, describes a kiln somewhat like this kiln, especially in reference to the "bench."

In the will of Phillip Bechard, written on June 11, 1822, he makes provision for both sons—among whom his 125-acre farm was to be divided—to have equal use of the kiln.

Several other interesting provisions of the will regarding the use of the stream along the property may be found in the discussion of Shirk's Meadow Lime Kiln (No. 84).

Caernarvon Township. Topo. Kiln No. 35. N40.132865 W75.949876.

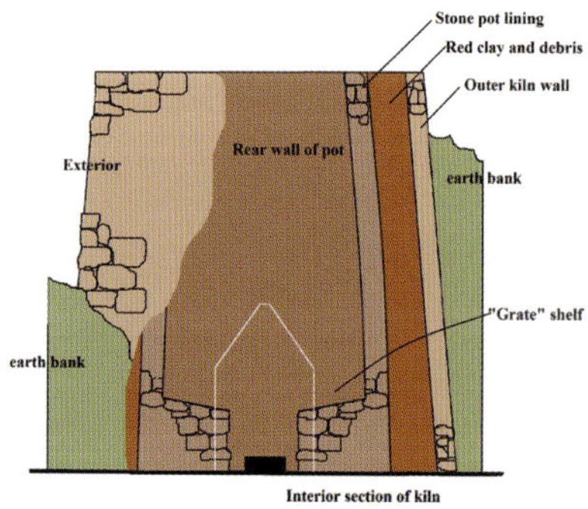

Schematic of the Shirk kiln, showing the location of stone ledges on either side of the fire trench, upon which iron bars were laid to support the charge.

Nos. 36, 37, and 38: Maxwell's Hill Lime Kilns

Maxwell's Hill Lime Kilns (Nos. 36, 37, and 38)

36

37

38

Midway between Churchtown and Morgantown, a set of four white silos and sheds may be seen standing in an abandoned quarry on the south side of Route 23. This was the quarrying and lime-burning business founded by Amos J. Stoltzfus, known as Maxwell's Hill Bluestone Quarry.

This enterprising Amish farmer began burning lime in 1928 in an old kiln on his farm. Two years later he built his first new kiln and shed in the quarry near the road. Before long, two more kilns were added and were later modified into draw kilns, giving the operation a capacity of producing up to 24 tons of lime per day.

An article in the *Honey Brook Herald* identified it as the only commercial lime-burning facility in the area. Its last fires went out as recently as 1971.

Amos Stoltzfus lived in the old farmhouse not far from the quarry and kilns. The following story was told to the author by Amos's grandson:

> Amos secretly purchased a handgun for the purpose of shooting vermin on the farm. Now some of these old farm houses often originally had the sheet-metal stovepipe running from the kitchen stove up through the floor and out through a clay liner high up in the bedroom wall. In later years, when a central heating system was installed, the chimney hole was covered over with a tin plate, often corrugated around the edge with a picture in the middle.
>
> Amos—a little guilty about having the revolver in the house—hid it in the chimney hole behind the plate. One day a daughter, while cleaning the room, removed the plate, and there was the gun.
>
> Well, when the story got out, Amos immediately got the gun, took it up to the lime kilns, where they were building a shed, and dropped it down into the hollow cement blocks of the partially built wall. The wall was finished and the gun should be there today!

His grandson tells me that he has a pretty good idea where it would be, and hopes he's around when they someday tear down the old buildings.

Lime was produced and stored in these sheds and silos. The three kilns pictured are inside the sheds. The silos were used to store grain after the lime kiln fires went out.

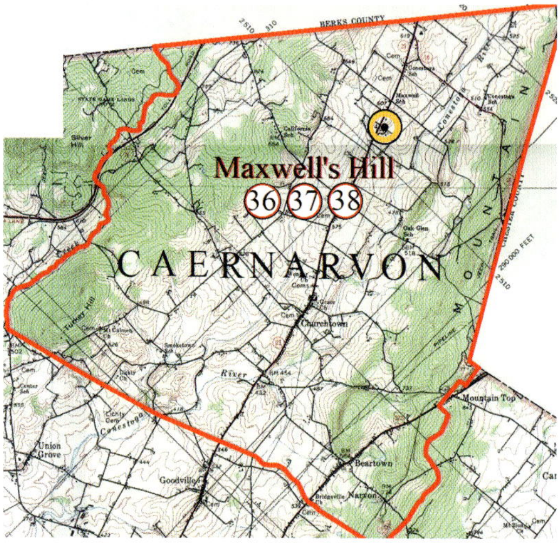

Caernarvon Township. Topo. Kiln Nos. 36, 37, and 38. N40.144653 W75.921206.

No. 39: "The Friendly Ram" Lime Kiln

39

Like a Judean tomb tucked into the hillside, this kiln is hidden down off the roadside along Creek Road, three-quarters of mile north of Oregon Road (Route 722). Although it is built with a large, deep archway, its redeeming feature is related to the name we have given it, "the Friendly Ram." It's a story that emerged while I was photographing the kiln:

> My friend, Ed, told me about the old kiln adjacent to his farm and gave me directions to find it, hidden in the meadow. When I arrived I noticed across the meadow, as I hopped the gate, a small flock of sheep. While making my way along Lititz Spring Creek in search of the kiln, I felt something pushing against my hips. Looking down, there was this big old ram with curved horns walking along beside me. He seemed harmless enough. I scratched his head, and we conversed as we walked along together.
>
> When we reached the kiln, I told him, "Now you stay here. I want to take some pictures," and he stood there watching as I walked to the kiln. Then suddenly I felt a hefty bump on the rear—not enough to do any damage. Startled, I turned to him and said, "Hey! What are you doing? Cut that out," and went about my business.
>
> He stood watching as I got my photographs. Then I said, "OK, Come on now. Let's go back." Calmly he escorted me back to the gate just as before, then turned and without fanfare walked across the meadow to his flock.
>
> The next time I saw Ed, he said seriously, "Oh, I forgot to tell you, there is a mad sheep in that meadow by the kiln." I smiled and he added, "No fooling, he chased some fisherman into the creek and broke one fellow's leg. He's bad news." "Oh, him," I chuckled. "He and I are good friends."
>
> A few month later I saw Ed again. He said, "Hey, they got rid of that mad sheep." Sadly I replied, "I'm sorry to hear that. You know, I may have been the only friend he ever had."

"The Friendly Ram" Lime Kiln (No. 39)

A "friendly ram" (*Ovis aires*)

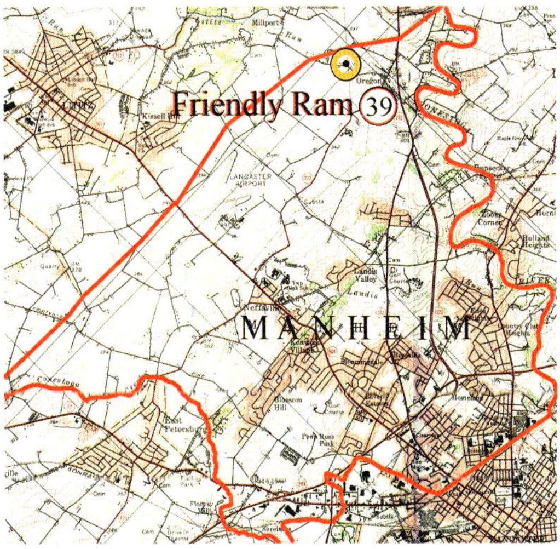

Manheim Township. Topo. Kiln No. 39. N40.121505 W76.254020.

No. 40: Amish Farm and House Lime Kiln

40

Amish House and Farm Lime Kiln (No. 40)

The waterwheel cable attached to the well pump

This lime kiln is hidden behind the Target store in the shopping center along one of the busiest sections of Route 30 East. It is on the grounds of the Amish Farm and House—a popular tourist attraction—a small, authentic Lancaster County farmstead that is restored to parklike conditions.

The barn was built in 1803, and one of the curators thought that the kiln may have been built about that time, but we do not find it marked on either the 1864 or 1875 atlas, suggesting that it was of later construction.

The metal roof is a modern addition, although they did often construct a covering, sometimes temporarily, over the kiln during the burn. The kiln is small as far as our county kilns go, being but 20 feet across the front and 9 feet to the top.

An interesting feature is shown (*right*). Along the small stream not far from the kiln is an enclosed waterwheel. The attached cable runs uphill to the "Amish" house, where it operates an old-fashioned hand pump, a system that was found on many farms in earlier times.

The waterwheel apparatus, showing the cable that operates a hand pump on the house porch approximately 130 yards uphill

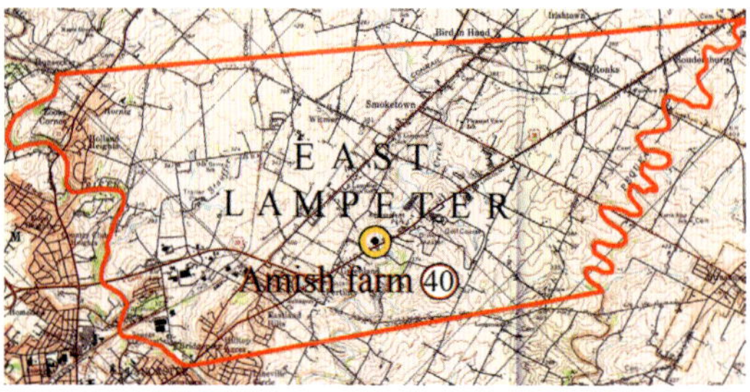

AEast Lampeter Township. Topo. Kiln No. 40. N40.030404 W76.229522.

No. 41: Kinderhook Road Gothic Lime Kiln

Kinderhook Road Gothic Lime Kiln (No. 41)

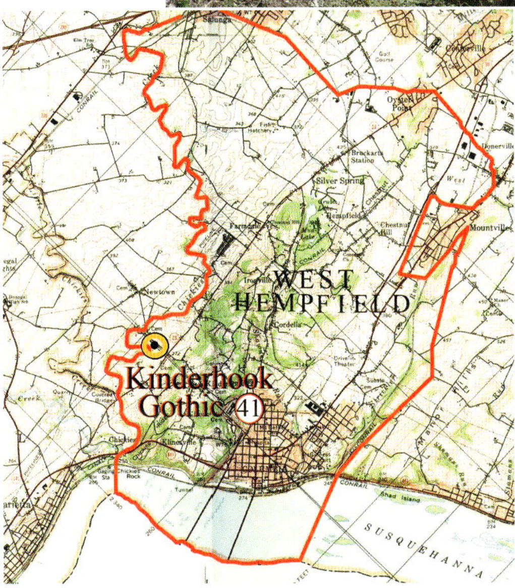

West Hempfield Township. Topo. Kiln No. 41. N40.065269 W76.499218.

This delightful example of industrial archeology may be found partially hidden in the summertime by overhanging foliage on the west side of Kinderhook Road, a quarter of a mile north of Route 23.

A heavy carpet of moss enhances the rustic beauty of this attractive and unusual lime kiln. Few lime burners or masons would go to the trouble of constructing their kiln with such a charming Gothic arch.

Another interesting and decorative feature is the offset of the upper three or four courses of stone at the top. The kiln appears to have been designed by an artist, one who would no doubt be pleased with its ancient appearance today.

Note also that the rear of the archway is closed off, leaving a very small draw hole at the bottom, barely adequate to ignite the fires and rake out the burnt lime. The Chiques Creek loops its way behind the kiln, with several attractive covered bridges nearby.

Siegrest Mill Covered Bridge over Chiques Creek in West Hempfield Township

No. 42: Longenecker Road Lime Kiln

42

Near Mount Joy—a little less than a half mile south from East Main Street (Route 230)—along Longenecker Road we find this classic bluestone lime kiln.

While the exterior is handsomely designed and built, the inside burning chamber, or pot, oddly does not form a complete stone circle; it is more like a horseshoe, with the back blending into the earthen bank. A further mystery is that the walls of the pot are not lined with the typical fieldstone or sandstone. This is highly unusual, since the stones would have themselves burned into lime along with the rest of the charge.

Furthermore, the insides of the stones are not mortared or coated with plaster or mud. Neither do they show any signs of burning. In the small photo we can see that the outer walls resemble a facade that was never meant to be a functioning lime kiln. Perhaps it was never finished; it appears, instead, to have been planned to be a giant lawn ornament!

Longenecker Road Lime Kiln (No. 42)

Rapho Township. Topo. Kiln No. 42. N40.103321 W76.491128.

The kiln from the rear, showing the unfinished half-round pot

No. 43: Musser Road Lime Kiln

43

Musser Road Lime Kiln (No. 43)

This handsome kiln is built into the bank alongside Musser Road, approximately a mile south of Route 230 and the town of Florin.

It appears carefully and attractively designed, with a large, impressive brick arch and heavy "dovetailed" corners of a darker stone.

Bittersweet berries (*Solanum dulcomara*) growing in the rocks of the kiln

East Donegal Township. Topo. Kiln No. 43. N40.101098 W76.534723.

No. 44: Maytown Road Lime Kiln

44

Maytown Road Lime Kiln (No. 44)

Nestled in a nest of verdant green summer grasses, this lovely blue-limestone kiln faces Maytown Road directly across from a huge poultry house, a little short of a mile and a half north of the village of Maytown.

It is fairly well constructed of local blue limestone, with a contrasting red-brick archway that is unusually large, deep, and wide. Several fairly large trees growing on top of the kiln are an especially unwelcome sign.

Although it appears to be tucked into a woods, it is in fact surrounded by only a few trees in a relatively small woodlot. It is otherwise isolated in the open farmland of East Donegal Township (*see photo*), looking west from the kiln toward the setting sun perched like a glowing candle atop a distant silo beyond a field of golden wheat in the foreground.

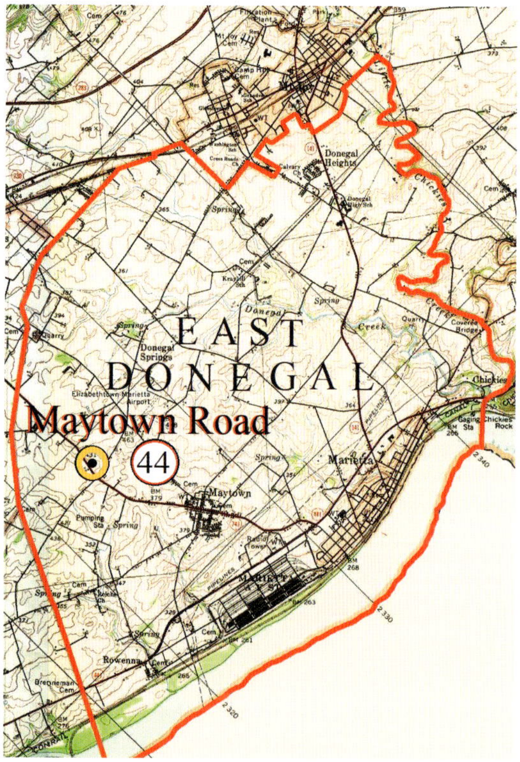

East Donegal Township. Topo. Kiln No. 44. N40.093359 W76.591476.

The setting sun over the East Donegal farmland in front of the kiln

No. 45: Silver Mine Lime Kiln

45

Silver Mine Lime Kiln (No. 45)

The sealed entrance to the old silver mine passageways

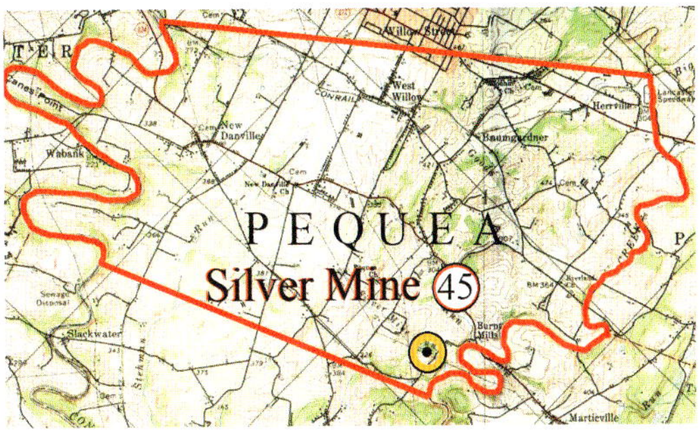

Pequea Township. Topo. Kiln No. 45. N39.945289 W76.313101.

This large, crisply restored lime kiln is along the path north of the parking lot in Pequea Township's Silver Mine Park, which is along Silver Mine Road approximately half a mile west of Marticville Road.

It is especially tall, at 25 feet from the base to the top of the kiln, compared to an average of 14 feet for most kilns. The exceptionally long log lintel forming the top of the arch is composed of three logs nearly 11 feet in length.

About 100 yards beyond the kiln is the *adit* or entrance to the old silver mine for which the park is named. Before the township purchased the property, the mine entrance was open to exploration by generations of young people, as well as occasional professional geologists and scientists. Several vertical shafts filled to the floor level with water make the experience of exploring the cave-like tunnels all the more inviting. In the 1960s, several scuba divers went down into them but succeeded only in stirring up a lot of mud. Cave-adapted invertebrates such as white planaria and isopods have been reported in the water.

The ruins of a second kiln (No. 89) are hidden in the shadow at the lower right of the picture.

Trail maps and an excellent geology guide written by Dr. Donald Wise of Franklin and Marshall College are available at the parking lot and may also be found on the internet at www.pequeatwp.org/wp-content/uploads/2014/02/Pequea-Township-Park-Geology-Guide.pdf.

Nos. 46 and 47: Martin's Grove Lime Kilns

46

47

Martin's Grove Lime Kilns (Nos. 46 and 47)

Along a stand of trees known as Martin's Grove, these two lime kilns are tucked into the southeast corner of the intersection of Routes 222 and 322, just east of Ephrata Borough.

Although this lime kiln is basically in fairly sound condition, a considerable number of rocks have tumbled from the upper walls. There is evidence of a third kiln off the picture to the right, in the form of a depression in the bank and a pile of rocks. The Martin family maintains the area above and in front of the kilns as a picnic grove.

Kiln No. 47 on the right (*small photo*) is the only kiln found that has the iron retaining bars still in the draw hole. Usually they are removed when the kiln is emptied of quicklime.

Kiln No. 47 (*right*), showing five iron retaining bars still remaining in the draw hole

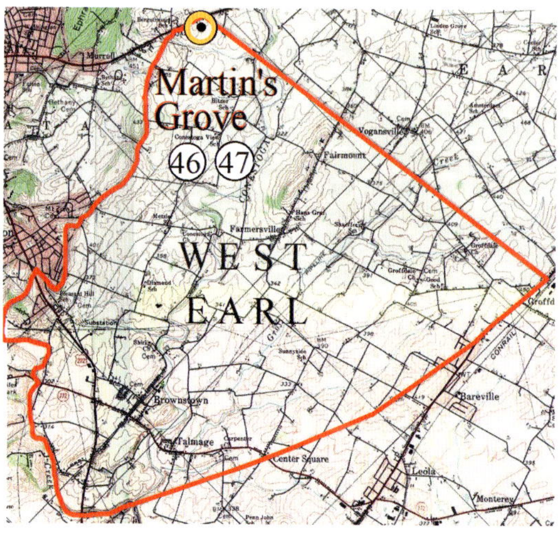

West Earl Township. Topo. Kiln No. 46. N40.159016 W76.150548.

No. 48: Pequea Creek Road Lime Kiln

48

Pequea Creek Road Lime Kiln (No. 48)

Woodsia ferns (*on the left*), fragile fern (*on the right*)

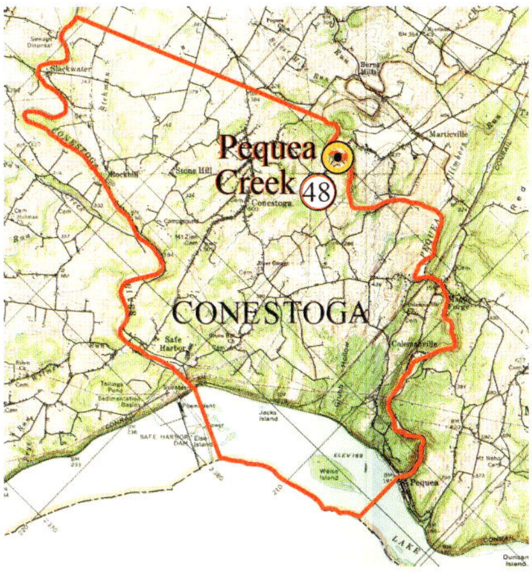

Conestoga Township. Topo. Kiln No. 48. N39.923217 W76.326676.

This neat-looking limestone kiln is another that is "well hidden in plain view"! When you are traveling north on Pequea Creek Road, approximately 1.5 miles from River Road, a low stone wall (*below*) may be seen alongside the road, overlooking Pequea Creek. Though the road passes within 20 feet of this wall, few would guess that it is the top of a lime kiln.

When viewed from below (*above*) we can see that it is solidly built of limestone and has been well maintained over the years. Sometime in the not-too-distant past, the arch was re-inforced with a new heavy wooden beam.

Two superficially similar species of wall ferns decorate the face of the kiln. Blunt-lobed woodsia has light-green scaly stems, whereas those of fragile fern are dark green to black and wirelike (the stem referred to is in reality the basal part of the leaf or frond, which is known as the stipe, the true stem being underground or in the crevices of the rocks in this case).

View from the road, showing the kiln extending above the grade as a low wall

1. Blunt-lobed woodsia (*Woodsia obtusa*)

2. Woodsia stalk, showing plentiful whitish scales

3. Fragile fern (*Cystopteris fragilis*)

4. *Cystopteris* stalk, showing dark brown near the base and turning green above

5. Heart-shaped gametophytes, which develop from spores and give rise to the frond (sporophyte)

6. Base of fragile fern, showing development of a young sporophyte

7. "Daddy long legs" spider (*Pholcus phalangioides*), which appears to be missing one of its eight legs

8. Rare pink "pillbug" that had just shed its skin (*lower right*) near the smaller, normal gray-colored form

Spiderweb burrow, commonly found in the stone joints of old kilns

Small slug making its way up the rocks of the kiln

No. 49: Metzler's Road Lime Kiln

Metzler's Road Lime Kiln (No. 49)

This large, recently restored lime kiln is hidden behind the sheds of a private residence along Metzler's Road, approximately 300 yards north of the Conestoga River and a mile and a half north of Farmersville in West Earl Township.

The small photo (*below*) shows the kiln in 2008, prior to restoration. Trees cause the most-severe damage to even our most well-built kilns.

Photo taken in 2008, before restoration

This kiln has an unusually deep concave front, curving back nearly 2 feet at the middle. Presumably this was done to stabilize the kiln and prevent it from pushing outward. Most kilns do not show this much curvature. The kiln is broad, measuring 22 feet across the front, but the draw arch is especially small at approximately 3 feet high and wide.

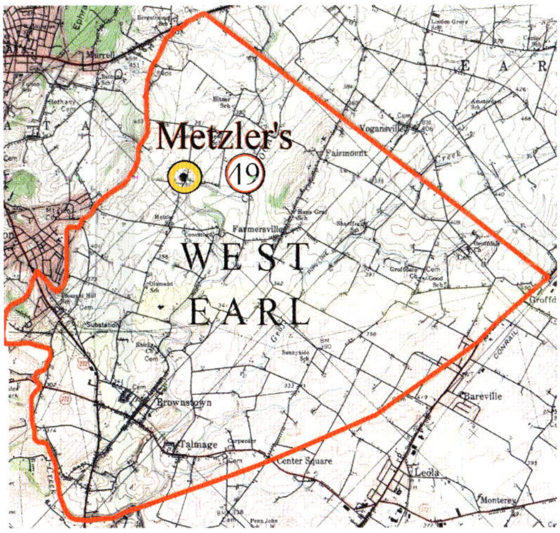

West Earl Township. Topo. Kiln No. 49. N40.146123 W76.169499.

50

No. 50: Lime Rock Road Lime Kiln

Lime Rock Road Lime Kiln (No. 50)

Blunt-lobed woodsia covering the front of the kiln

Hidden on a rocky, wooded hillside a quarter mile west of W. Middle Creek Road and midway between Wissler Road and Lime Rock Road in Clay Township, this kiln has several features of interest.

The face of the kiln is concave, as noted at the top, which clearly curves inward. No doubt the builders thought this would strengthen the front, keeping it from pushing out. Then there is an interesting wall along the right side, whose function seems to be none other than strengthening that side of the kiln, which is well exposed aboveground. It is not tied into the main structure, suggesting it was likely added later, possibly after it began to push outward. The close-up of the arch shows that the lintel is a huge, flat limestone slab approximately 4 feet square, covering most of the "roof" of the archway.

The front of the kiln, facing north, is always shaded and supports a large population of a small rock fern known as blunt-lobed woodsia.

Close-up showing the huge limestone slab lintel extending back into the archway

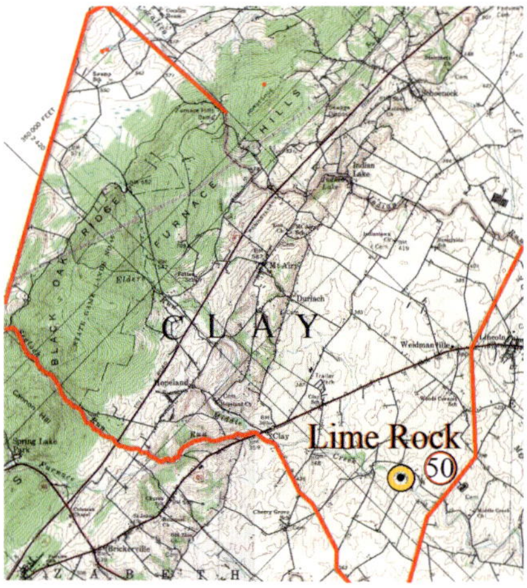

Clay Township. Topo. Kiln No. 50. N40.196568 W76.243567.

No. 51: Weaver Farm Lime Kiln

51

Weaver Farm Lime Kiln (No. 51)

In a small hillside copse surrounded by brush and trees, roughly 150 yards across the fields from North Churchtown Road, we find this solid sandstone *kalik offe* that looks like it was built to stand for centuries.

Though now partially hidden by a trash dump, if cleaned up and maintained it would make a picturesque monument on the hill, overlooking a small meandering stream in the meadow below. Below we can see how the massive sandstone blocks continue back into the archway, topped by a large stone lintel like a smaller version of the front arch and creating the similarly shaped draw hole leading into the pot. Kilns similar to this are more common in the northern and eastern parts of the county and in neighboring Chester County.

Looking toward the back of the archway and the matching smaller draw hole

Caernarvon Township. Topo. Kiln No. 51. N40.147476 W76.990464.

No. 52: Walnut Run Lime Kiln

52

Walnut Run Lime Kiln (No. 52)

Deteriorating log and stone corbelled back of the archway, supported by an iron lintel over the small, square draw hole

This formidable, fortresslike lime kiln is hidden in a small grove of trees in the middle of otherwise open farmland 400 yards southwest of the intersection of Lime Valley Road and Bachman Road in Strasburg Township.

It is constructed with massive blocks of finely stratified limestone that have minimal distortions or inclusions, almost resembling poured concrete. The huge lintel over the draw arch is 8.5 feet long, 1 foot thick, and 2 feet wide, equaling 17 cubic feet of very solid limestone. If we use a standard weight of limestone at 175 pounds per cubic foot, this block alone would weigh 1.5 tons (Delaware Quarries, Inc., New Hope, Pennsylvania); it would have been an enormous undertaking to construct this kiln in the late 1800s. The limestone blocks are very light colored, with the surface darkening and green from a heavy growth of algae and moss, resulting from constant summer shade and eastern exposure.

Strasburg Township. Topo. Kiln No. 52. N39.960954 W76.215623.

No. 53: "Deafy's Den" Lime Kiln

53

"Deafy's Den" Lime Kiln (No. 53). *Hobo inserted by the author after Rockwell 1924*

Snapshot of the kiln from the 1940s. *Courtesy of Gordan Sneath, whose family stands in the arch*

Invisible from the field above, this classic-looking kiln sits at the top of a steep, wooded hillside overlooking Little Conestoga Creek some 80 feet below. It's "way back at the edge of the trees" on a farm along Walnut Hill Road, a little less than a mile and a half south of Millersville. As if time stood still, there seems to have been little change since the old photo of the family in the arch was taken in the 1940s. Even the locust posts, now fallen to the ground, were standing by the arch more than seventy years ago. "Deafy's Den" was named by the children who occasionally slipped away from the nearby schoolhouse for quick visits with the friendly, hard-of-hearing old hobo who sometimes made it his home, according to Gordon Sneath, who was one of those children. Here his visage made a surprise visit for our photo! (Deafy's reincarnation was modified from a Norman Rockwell painting that appeared on the cover of the *Saturday Evening Post* on October 18, 1924; Curtis Publishing Company.)

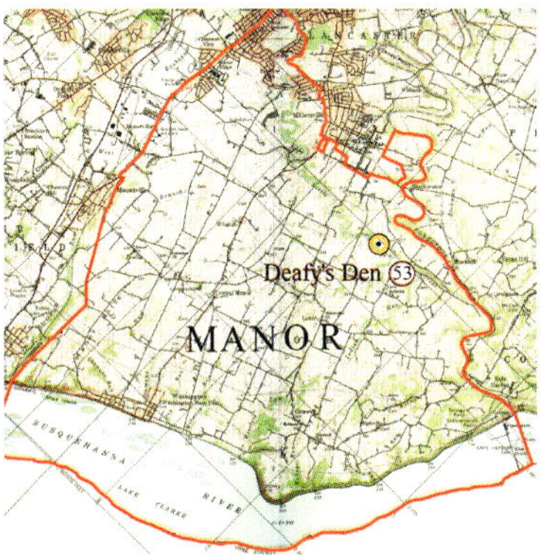

Manor Township. Topo. Kiln No. 53. N39.919397 W76.376575.

Archway into "Deafy's Den"

Cushion of one of the various species of moss growing on the kiln

Hinge of a door used to close off the kiln during a burning

Ebony spleenwort fern

"Deafy's" view from inside the archway

A "spider's den" on "Deafy's den"

No. 54: Hawkins's Woods Lime Kiln

Hawkins's Woods Lime Kiln (No. 54)

This vine-enshrouded blue-limestone kiln with a huge archway is hidden deep in the woods of southern Conestoga Township, between the Susquehanna River and River Hill Road.

These now-wooded hills were once farms of several families, with remnants of old foundations still found nearby. The 1875 county atlas shows buildings of Jacob Brenneman and Andrew Wise not far from the kiln. What is now a vast second-growth forest was once home to Benedict Eshleman, a 1720 Swiss immigrant who left his mark throughout southern Lancaster County with several large handsome mansions. He is buried not far from the lime kiln in a large family cemetery hidden atop the wooded hills nearby.

A few hundred yards away is Bausman's Hollow, which was the site of the infamous McAbee Dynamite Factory, which on July 9, 1909, at 12:42 exploded with a tremendous force, blowing everything to smithereens and instantly killing eleven of the workers. The blast was so ferocious that the bodies had to be gathered up in pieces and buried in a single casket at the Colemanville Methodist Church cemetery.

The dynamite factory before the explosion. *Photo credit, Michael Froil blog: michaelfroil.wordpress.com/2013/05/30/shenks-ferry; source: Collection of Columbia Historical Preservation Society*

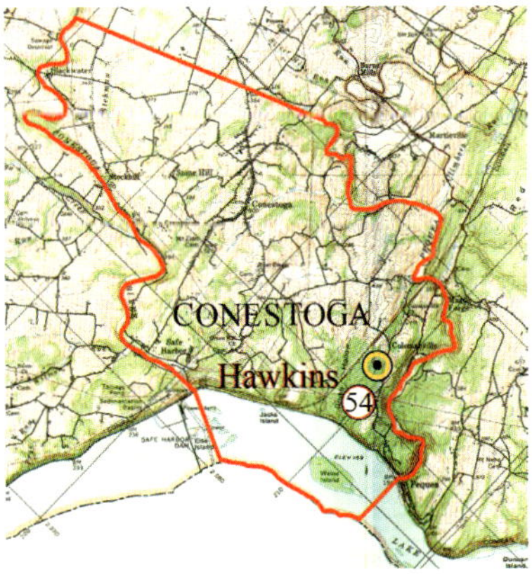

Conestoga Township. Topo. Kiln No. 54. N39.904966 W76.355689.

No. 55: Strickland's Lime Kiln

55

Strickland's Lime Kiln (No. 55)

This green-encrusted sandstone lime kiln rests against a low bank overlooking a small brook meandering through the farmland below.

It is green because it faces northwesterly, away from the sun, with the stones perpetually in the shade, where algae, lichen, and moss can find it a favorable substrate. It appears that approximately 4 feet of the right side was laid up with large rocks sometime after the original construction, probably to stabilize that end.

The long log lintel (*below*) is in an advanced state of decay and about to give way, and when it does, the entire middle section of the kiln will come crashing down with it. This is an example of the aging and neglect that threatens many of our county kilns.

Decaying log lintel, threatening the survival of the kiln

Conoy Township. Topo. Kiln No. 55. N40.103572 W76.642970.

No. 56: Sunrise Lime Kiln

Sunrise Lime Kiln (No. 56)

Easter sunrise service (undated snapshot, ca. 1950s)

Looking very much like a biblical tomb in the garden, this somewhat over-restored kiln is at the rear of a property at the corner of River Road and Safe Harbor Road, a quarter mile west of Conestoga Boulevard.

The concrete reinforcement has surely stabilized the kiln, although it does detract from the historical design. The small image is from an old, undated snapshot—possibly about 1950—during an Easter sunrise service, before those modifications were made, which suggested the name.

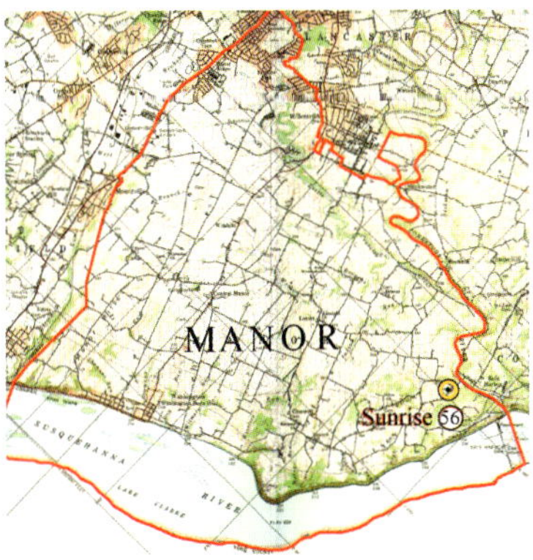

Manor Township. Topo. Kiln No. 56. N39.939862 W76.391446.

No. 57: White Horse Lime Kiln

57

White Horse Lime Kiln (No. 57)

The 1740 White Horse Inn

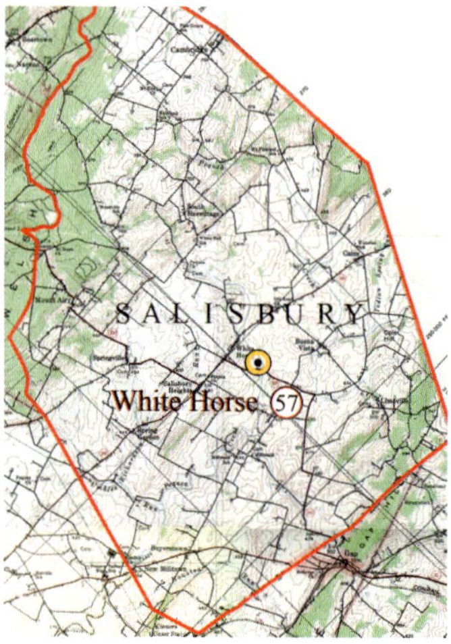

Salisbury Township. Topo. Kiln No. 57. N40.029777 W75.994500.

This rustic kiln is in Salisbury Township, about half a mile south of the village of White Horse. It is well hidden behind some farm buildings in a grove of trees 400 yards east of White Horse Road.

Salisbury Township was once a hotbed of lime burning. A circle with a radius of 2.5 scale miles drawn on the 1875 Lancaster County atlas from the geographical center of the township includes thirty-five lime kilns. This kiln was not one of them, apparently built after the survey for that year. Old deeds show that the farm was owned by a David Stoltzfus shortly after that time, and he possibly built and used the kiln.

The nearby White Horse Hotel (now an inn) was built long before the lime kiln (1740) by Sarah and John Clemson, who secured the original patent from the Penns. It is considered to be the oldest continuously operated hotel in Lancaster County and would have entertained most of the travelers passing west from Philadelphia on the Old Conestoga Road. Accordingly, George and Martha Washington are said to have slept here on their way to Lancaster when it was the US capitol for a day (September 27, 1777) and the Continental Congress had fled from the British, who had captured Philadelphia.

Nos. 58a and 58b: Bamboo Grove Lime Kilns

Bamboo Grove Lime Kilns (Nos. 58a and 58b)

Tall, narrow draw hole of Kiln No. 58a

Arch of Kiln No. 58b

This moss-encrusted red-sandstone kiln is well concealed in a stand of bamboo and brush behind a metalworking shop, 220 yards west of Railroad Avenue and 0.6 miles south of Route 322.

A layer of concrete was at one time poured along the top of the kiln to stabilize it. This feature and the fact that no trees are growing on top have contributed to its survival in very good condition.

A second draw arch to the left is fairly intact, although the stonework above that arch has been demolished. Both draw arches are supported by heavy iron plates and bars. The draw hole of the main kiln is unusually tall and narrow, being a mere 8 inches wide at the top and more than 36 inches tall. It is oddly angled to the left as it opens into the pot. The property was owned by Christian S. Kurtz as late as 1932.

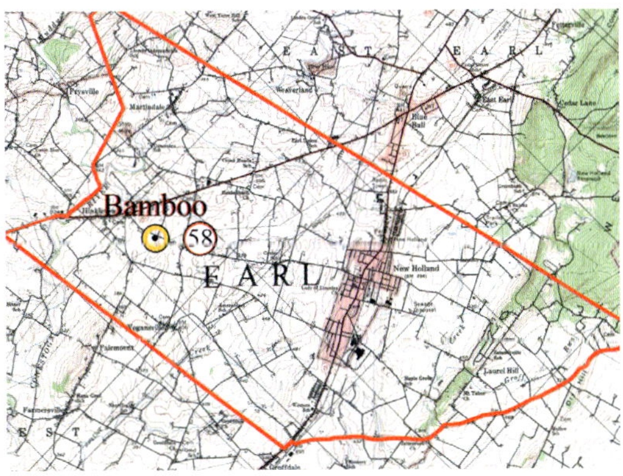

Earl Township. Topo. Kiln No. 58. N40.136068 W76.117016.

No. 59: Cook's Landing Lime Kiln

59

Cook's Landing Lime Kiln (No. 59)

This fascinating lime kiln is unusual for its extreme concave front curvature of 4 feet. Surprisingly, the huge, dense mica schist lintel is also concavely carved. It is always amazing how the old timers maneuvered these heavy stones into place. This lintel measures 52 × 17 × 13 inches. With mica schist having an average specific gravity of 2.6, the lintel would weigh about half a ton. The arch would extend down another 2–3 feet behind the dirt and debris in front.

This kiln is along Cook's Landing Road, a half mile south of the intersection with Grubbs Corner Road in the extreme southeastern corner of Lancaster County, where it once provided burnt lime for the "southern end."

It is unusual to find a lime kiln in Fulton Township, since the limestone deposits do not extend much farther south than Quarryville. The answer is that the limestone was brought downriver from York County in barges or "arks," then across to Peach Bottom and other sites such as Cook's Landing and hauled uphill to the kiln. This was apparently a better solution than hauling the stone south by wagon from Quarryville.

Less than 100 yards behind the kiln is this lovely stone mansion built in the very early 1800s by William Cook, prominent patriarch of the Cook family here in the southern end, some of whom were involved in the transport and burning of lime.

William Cook's Mansion, about 100 yards behind the kiln

Fulton Township. Topo. Kiln No. 59. N39.725850 W76.212266.

Cook's Scenic railroad tunnel near Cook's Landing

Swallowtail butterflies "puddling" at the base of the cliff near the tunnel

Feral pigeons roosting in the tunnel

Blunt-lobed woodsia with ebony spleenwort at the base

View across the wide Susquehanna near Cook's Landing

No. 60: Mann's Creek Lime Kiln

Mann's Creek Lime Kiln (No. 60)

View into the old arch, showing the small draw hole in the back

This slowly deteriorating kiln is hidden away on a wooded bank along the winding West Branch of Little Conestoga Creek, 225 yards north of Bender Mill Road.

Time has taken its toll on the derelict, whose stones appear to have been laid up without mortar. It's always surprising to find these old log lintels having survived more than a hundred years. Trees growing on the top on the other hand always take their toll.

Manor Township. Topo. Kiln No. 60. N39.994236 W76.406108.

No. 61: Gideon's Lime Kiln

Gideon's Lime Kiln (No. 61)

Potato storage bin inside the renovated kiln

This interesting structure is in a bank 175 yards south of the intersection of School Lane and White Horse Road (Route 897).

Several years ago the owner showed me the remains of this kiln, completely buried under trash and soil, so that only a few stones were exposed aboveground. Then his son began building a house nearby, within 100 feet of the kiln. He knew the kiln was down there, and during the excavation uncovered it, with the idea of putting it back into use, though not for burning lime—he had other ideas in mind. First he poured a slab of concrete over the top, and that became the base for a small pavilion. Then they thoroughly cleaned out the inside, had the stones pointed, and sprayed the ceiling with insulation. Now this relic that served previous generations of lime burning has been completely resurrected into a new life, this time as a potato cellar.

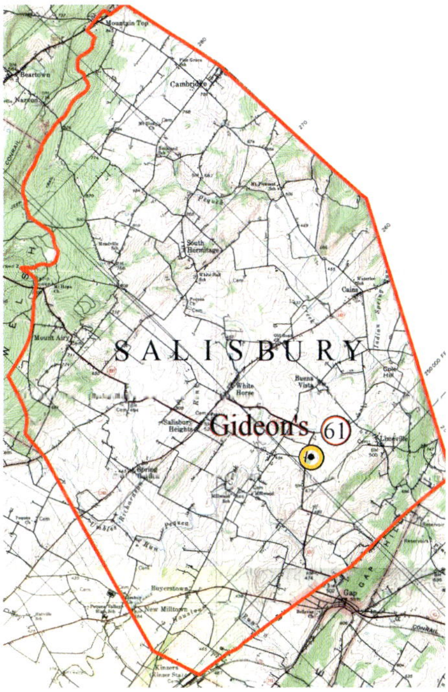

Salisbury Township. Topo. Kiln No. 61. N40.011528 W75.995816.

Nos. 62, 63, and 64: Quarryville Lime Kilns

62

63

64

Quarryville Lime Kilns (Nos. 62, 63, and 64)

This wonderful set of lime kilns was a surprising discovery. The kilns are well hidden and relatively inaccessible, so only a handful of people know about them. And yet they sit, silently waiting to be rediscovered in the woods near the railroad tracks just northeast of the borough of Quarryville. The kiln on the left bears the only date stone found in this study. On the front left section, about head high, the date "JUNE 11, 1879" is clearly carved into a large stone, presumably the day that construction was completed. The 1875 atlas shows twenty lime kilns within 1.25 miles of downtown Quarryville. *Our Quarryville*, an online newsletter, cites the *Ledger Newspapers* (October 16, 1991) in stating that in Quarryville at one time, "there were 40 lime-kilns in place, producing annually 500,000 barrels of lime and employing 100 men." These three kilns were presumably not included in these counts. Today they are the only ones known in the immediate Quarryville area. Small holes, possibly for ventilation, are clearly visible near the bottom of the kilns. This is a feature we have not seen on other kilns.

A deed in the Lancaster County Courthouse, dated April 1, 1880, describes the transfer of a tract of 54 acres of land on this site from Jacob M. Eckman to David Keen, part of a larger tract conveyed to Eckman in 1852 (Lancaster County Deed Book L11:527). The kilns are noted in the following clause:

> together with the right to the said David Keen his heirs and assigns forever, to travel on the road leading from the Valley Road through the land of the said Jacob M. Eckman and Amos Greist to the Drywells Road, on the road now made and all other persons having business at the limestone quarry or Kilns.

Date stone of 1879 on the front of Kiln No. 62

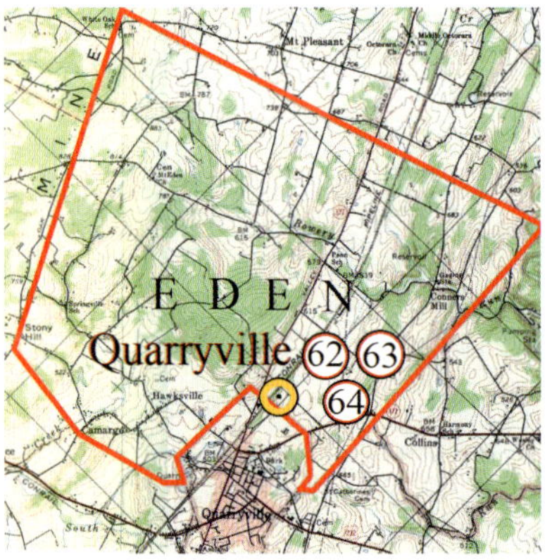

Eden Township. Topo. Kiln No. 62. N39.899988 W76.143953.

Nos. 65 and 66: Dicely Farm Lime Kilns

Dicely Farm Lime Kilns (Nos. 65 and 66)

This unmatched pair of lime kilns is the only such arrangement in the county. They were obviously built at different times, probably by different masons. We might speculate that the kiln on the left was built first, then some time later the second was added.

It appears the "new" kiln had to be extended several feet in front, and the pillar to its left was added to make a match.

Trees growing on top of these kilns is not unusual, but the maple in the upper left corner has been growing there for a long time, causing extensive damage. It is surprising that most of the kiln has not yet collapsed. This set of kilns is hidden behind an embankment at the southern perimeter of the development directly south of Long Park.

The kilns as seen from the south, across the meandering Little Conestoga on the creek trail in Dorwart Memorial Park

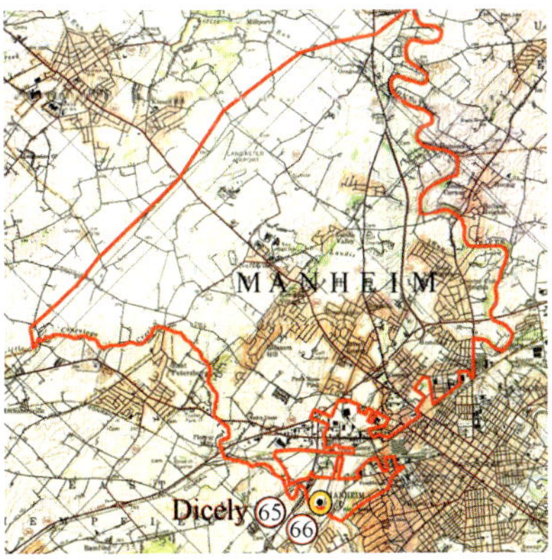

Manheim Township. Topo. Kiln No. 65. N40.057670 W76.341802.

67

No. 67: Martic Hill Lime Kiln

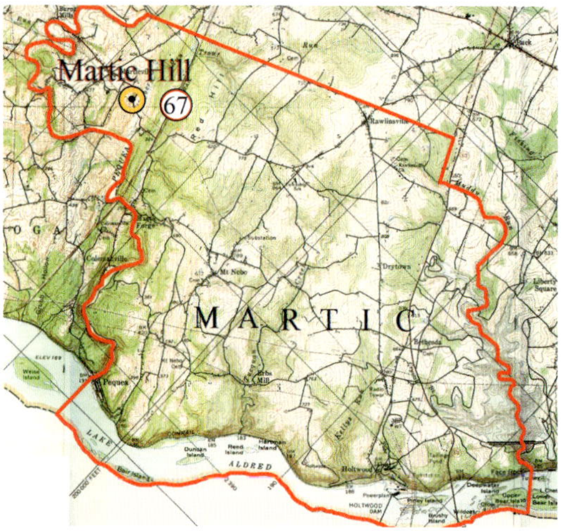

Martic Hill Lime Kiln (No. 67)

This attractive blue-limestone kiln would have to be rated, in just about every respect, among the top six or seven in the county. There is no evidence that it was ever rebuilt or restored, yet it looks like it was built yesterday.

It is highly visible along the berm of the road, where every day hundreds of cars pass within several feet of its lovely brick arch, 300 yards downhill (south) of the sharp right-angle turn in Route 724 between Marticville and Pennsy Road.

It is virtually a twin to the kiln on the Shertzer Farm (No. 1) along the Conestoga River just south of Millersville, near Slackwater. No other kilns in the county look so similar, suggesting they were almost certainly built by the same mason.

Middle: Shertzer's Meadow Lime Kiln (No. 1)

Bottom: Martic Township. Topo. Kiln No. 67. N39.919402 W76.307896.

No. 68: Parke Rohrer's Lime Kiln

68

Parke Rohrer's Lime Kiln (No. 68)

This deteriorating lime kiln is hidden along the edge of a woodland on the back end of a large dairy farm, a quarter mile south of Bunker Hill Road and about 200 yards west of a small Amish schoolhouse along Weaver Road.

Constructed of tan-colored sandstone, it was probably a nice-looking structure in its day. An interesting aspect of its design are the wings, which extend outward at a 45-degree angle on either side, similar to the kilns on Martin Barr Farm (No. 19) and the Pickle Farm (No. 13).

The gaping hole in the front is puzzling and hard to explain. It looks like the lintel in the center of the kiln was propped up with large stones before those on either side were pulled out, and yet some of them are still scattered about in front.

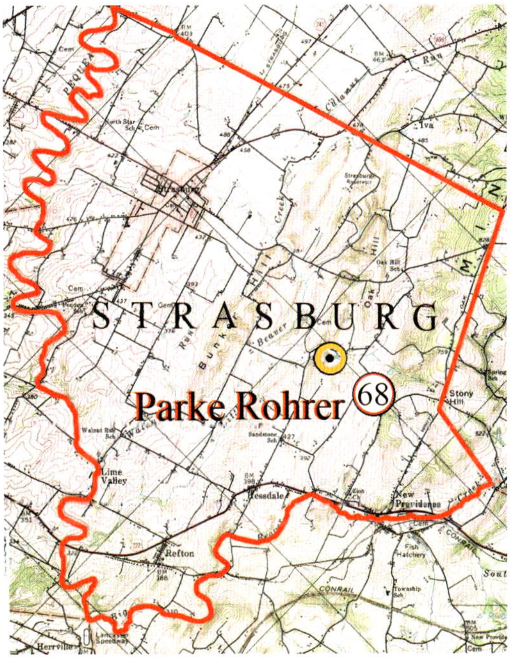

Strasburg Township. Topo. Kiln No. 68. N39.948598 W76.182191.

The kiln barely visible across the stream, at the edge of the woods

No. 69: Royer Road Lime Kiln

69

Royer Road Lime Kiln (No. 69)

This kiln is situated atop a steep hillside high above Conewago Creek, about 40 yards downstream from the bridge on Royer Road. The front is in precarious condition, and the arch has further collapsed since this photo was taken. It would seem that the entire center of the kiln may give way completely before long.

The upper middle of the front is strongly concave, possibly enabling the kiln to survive this long.

Location of the kiln high up on the bank above Cocalico Creek

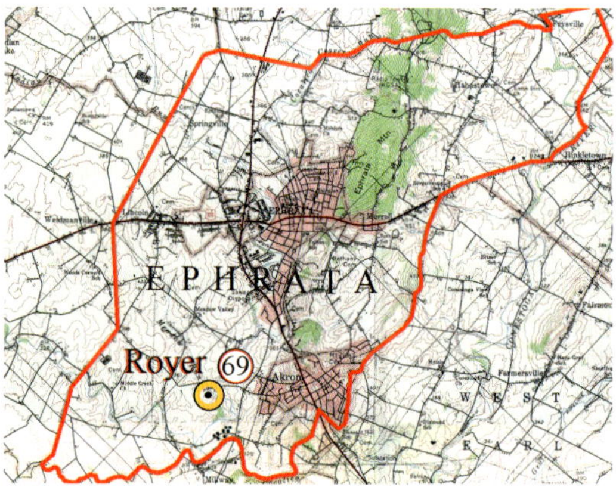

Ephrata Township. Topo. Kiln No. 69. N40.169434 W76.221096.

Nos. 70 and 71: Burkholder Lime Kilns

Burkholder Lime Kilns (Nos. 70 and 71)

The old waterwheel, long out of use

This attractive red-sandstone double kiln is hidden behind a large house 0.6 miles south of Frysville on Fry's Road. It is dug into the bank facing Muddy Creek and out of sight of the road.

The upper right corner of the front was expertly rebuilt several years ago. The property has been in Burkholder family hands since it was built in the early 1800s. Mr. Amos Hoover, historian and director of the Muddy Creek Library and Museum, says his grandfather David Burkholder burned lime here until 1928. He believes that the kiln was likely built by John E. Burkholder. Mr. Hoover has been a valuable resource for this project and relates the amusing story told here:

> It seems that Daniel Burkholder, deacon of the Weaverland Mennonite Church, accepted it his duty to be the first one at church Sunday morning so that he could open things up for his fellow worshippers. One fall weekend, some young lads thought to pull a trick on the deacon that they thought would interrupt his ritual. So late Saturday night they snuck into his carriage shed, jacked up his buggy, and removed all four wheels, rolling them downhill and into the open kiln, which had gone out of operation a generation before. But the joke turned on them.
>
> Daniel lived along the road above the kiln, and like many farmers who lived near flowing water, installed a contraption to operate a hand pump. Near the lime kiln a low-head dam was built across the creek that directed the water into a box with a waterwheel with a tall lever that oscillated back and forth. At the top a cable was attached that ran uphill to the hand pump on the porch. [One can see one of these devices still in operation at the Amish Home and Farm exhibit on Route 30, east of Lancaster.]
>
> Well, unbeknown to the boys, it was Daniel's practice to rise early in the morning and walk down to the waterwheel to clear it of any debris that may have washed in. It so happened that his path took him by the top of the old lime kiln, and he spied the wheels in the kiln and figured out what had happened. He patiently retrieved the wheels, remounted them on the buggy, had his breakfast, and was once again, to the chagrin of the red-faced culprits, the first one at church!

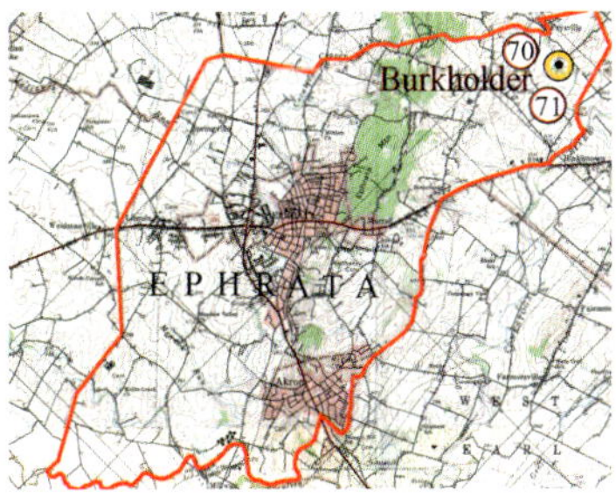

Ephrata Township. Topo. Kiln No. 70. N40.161760 W76.108046.

Nos. 72a and 72b: Rockhill Lime Kilns

72

Rockhill Lime Kilns (Nos. 72a and 72b)

This picturesque set of honeysuckle-shrouded bluestone arches sits at the edge of Stone Hill Road, around the corner about 100 yards from Long Lane and roughly 500 yards from the iron bridge at Rockhill.

At this crossing, a small group of dwellings and businesses once formed the community formerly known as Rockville. It included, in addition to a handful of houses, an inn, a blacksmith shop, a wagon shop, a woolen mill, a sawmill, a gristmill, and lime kilns, although it is unlikely they were the same kilns that are still present.

This is a little-known site of historical significance. It was the point at which Penn's land agent, James Logan, would have forded the stream to his post a short distance downstream on the other side. Among the travelers would have been William Penn and various dignitaries from Philadelphia traveling to the Indian village on the other side, as well as many of those traveling west.

An article in the Lancaster County Historical Records reads:

> In 1700 the main road westward from the little colony at Philadelphia was an Indian trail, leaving what is now Market Street, passing through Westchester, the Gap, the Long Lane, past [John] Postlewaite's trading post and tavern, crossing the Conestoga at Rock Hill (Lancaster County Historical Society Collection, xii, 146).

The iron bridge over the Conestoga River at Rockhill, 3 miles southwest of Millersville

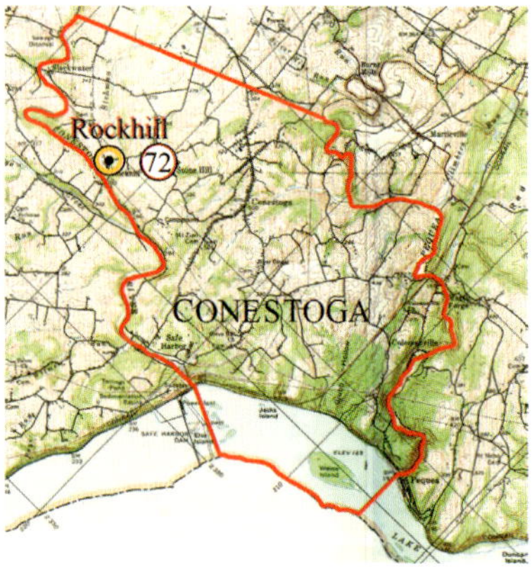

Conestoga Township. Topo. Kiln No. 72. N39.963355 W76.361542.

No. 73: Ramoth Lime Kilns

73

Former Ramoth Lime Kilns (No. 73), now demolished

Now demolished, this three-chambered commercial kiln was photographed in 2007, when this study began. It stood along the old Philadelphia and Reading Railroad tracks near the little community of Lime Rock, about 1.75 miles west of downtown Lititz.

An early deed shows that Dr. James Brobst, a prominent citizen and entrepreneur, purchased the property in 1879 and developed the stone and lime-burning business. It changed hands several times, eventually passing to the Ramoth Lime and Stone Company, which was listed in *The Ceramic Industries of Pennsylvania* (Shaw 1930) as one of 114 commercial lime producers in the state, on the basis of a survey in 1928, eight of which were in Lancaster County.

The business was liquidated in 1938, and the kilns were demolished sometime after 2007 by the Lititz Borough Maintenance Department. The small photo was taken in 2015 at approximately the same spot as the large one, showing how the kiln has been removed and the area filled and completely relandscaped, with no evidence of a kiln having ever been there.

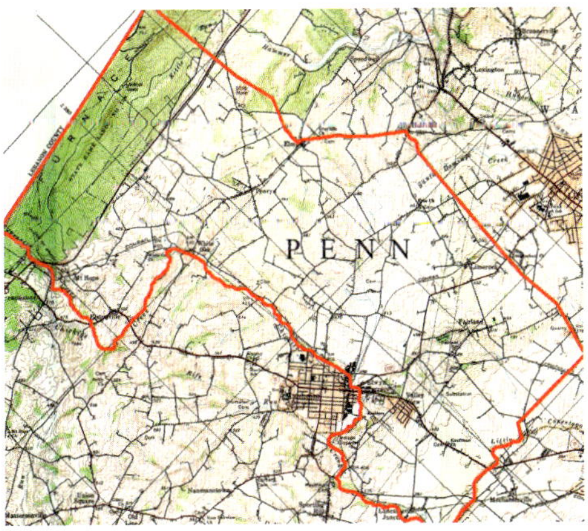

Penn Township. Topo. Kiln No. 73. N40.159206 W76.338368.

The site as it appears in 2017, after demolition of the kilns

No. 74: Sheepfold Lime Kiln

74

Sheepfold Lime Kiln (No. 74)

The lime kiln in its better days, probably the 1960s. *Courtesy, Dr. Joseph Glass, Millersville University*

The remains of this blue-limestone kiln are just north of the very narrow railroad underpass on Prospect Road, a half mile south of Route 462.

It is the only kiln in Lancaster County known to have a "dog-eared" peaked brick arch like a house roof. It is also one of the few rural lime kilns in the county where the pot is lined with fire brick. Unfortunately, a major portion of the front wall has since given way. One might speculate that this style of arch is less efficient in supporting the heavy stones above it; however, a close look at the ruins shows that the arch is still pretty much intact behind the pile of rubble that has fallen down from above. Above the arch the red-clay fill used to insulate the pot is clearly seen.

For a number of years during the late 1970s, there was a rustic fence in front of the kiln, enclosing a pen for several sheep that could find shelter underneath the arch; hence the name "Sheepfold."

The kiln looks sturdy enough in the earlier photo from the 1960s. With no trees on top and the arch seeming to be fairly intact, it is surprising that the front collapsed.

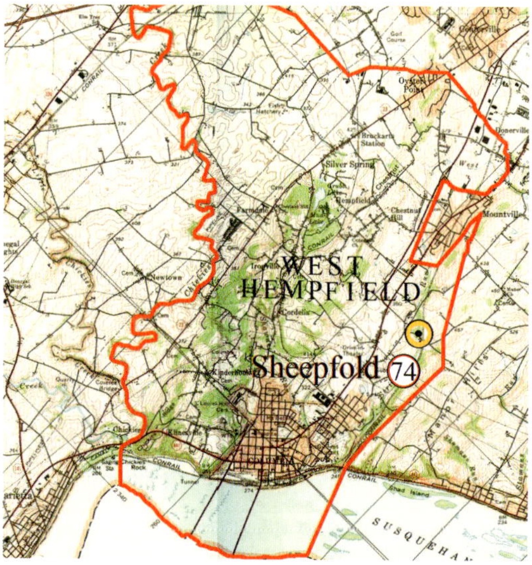

West Hempfield Township. Topo. Kiln No. 74. N40.029794 W76.455381.

No. 75: "White Mule" Lime Kiln

75

"White Mule" Lime Kiln (No. 75)

Possible date stone

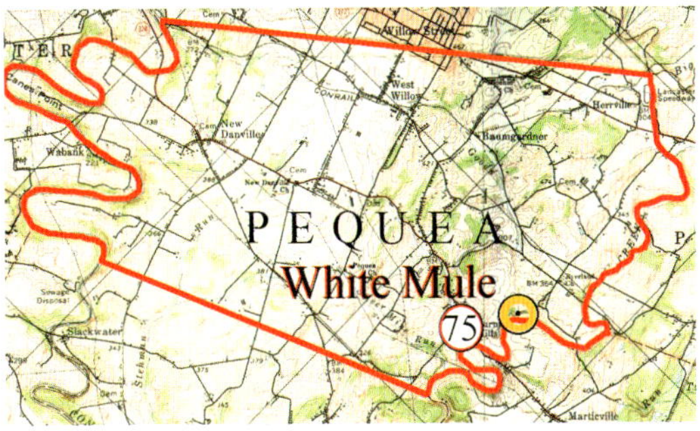

Pequea Township. Topo. Kiln No. 75. N39.940183 W76.201014.

Hidden on a wooded hillside some 35 feet above a large loop in Pequea Creek, 0.6 miles upstream from the bridge on Marticville Road, we find these ruins of a kiln.

Typical of many of these lime kilns— especially when a wooden lintel was used—the center arch is indicated by the straight sides to the main arch opening. High on the left sidewall there is a large cornerstone with what appears to be some numbers carved in it (1917?).

As usual, we know nothing about the kiln, but we can share a humorous story below, with a joke on the author, when he was visiting the kiln. The story, as one might guess, gave rise to the name:

> While searching for the kiln, we arrived at a farm along Byreland Church Road. The barn was built on a hill, with the stable on the upper level. When we parked below the barn, we noticed the picturesque scene of a white "horse" framed in the stable doorway above. Upon entering the stable, and securing permission from the young Amish farmer to hike back to the kiln for some photographs, I also asked if I could take a picture of his horse. He looked down, studied a bit, kicked at the manure, but didn't reply. Knowing the Amish shun being photographed, I said, "I'll be sure that you are not in the picture." He still hesitated, and I said again, "You wouldn't mind if I just took a picture of your horse, would you?" Whereupon he turned away, nodding toward the "horse," and said, "No, I guess I wouldn't mind you taking a picture of my horse, but that's a mule." I ducked out the door, headed for the kiln, and never did get my picture of the "horse."

No. 76: Lampeter Meadow Lime Kiln

76

Lampeter Meadow Lime Kiln (No. 76)

This rudely built and crumbling kiln sits near the edge of an old quarry (*visible at far left*) at the back (east side) of a farm meadow roughly 270 yards east of Mentzer Road and 900 yards north of Village Road (Route 741), East Lampeter Township.

The front of the arch is completely gone, with only the large stones stepped downward to the low horizontal draw hole. At least two of the stepped lintels are reinforced with iron bars. It appears that stones from time to time may come sliding down, so that soon there will be no wall at all. At some point the farmer will likely have it bulldozed away to clean up the meadow.

The arch, showing the flat stone lintels and the iron plates with the wide, low draw hole

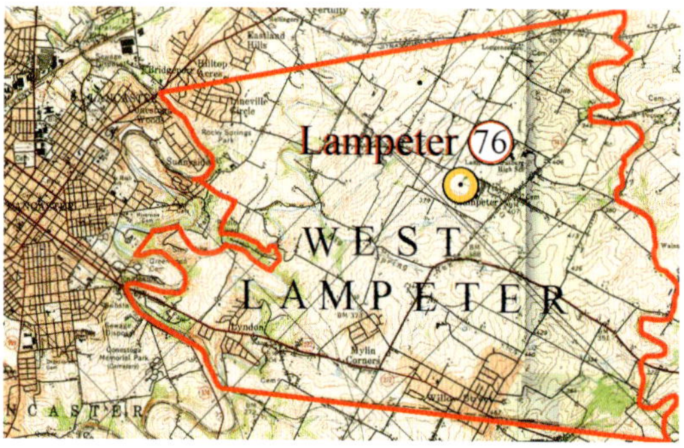

West Lampeter Township. Topo. Kiln No. 76. N39.997679 W76.247630.

No. 77: Mann's Ravine Lime Kiln

Mann's Ravine Lime Kiln (No. 77)

Blunt-lobed woodsia fern

Liverworts.

These remains may be found in a wooded ravine that runs downhill to Little Conestoga Creek, a quarter of a mile downstream from the bridge on Owl Bridge Road and a little more than a mile southwest of Millersville.

The kiln appears to have been well built, but once the main arch or lintel gives way, the center of these kilns collapses. Often this process is accelerated by trees growing on top of the kiln.

Even then, the ruins remain a picturesque remnant of our past. Some would call this a study in industrial archeology, or perhaps more appropriately agricultural archeology. The shaded crevices in the rocks of these old structures make excellent habitat for small, rock-loving plants such as the fern and liverworts pictured on the side of the kiln.

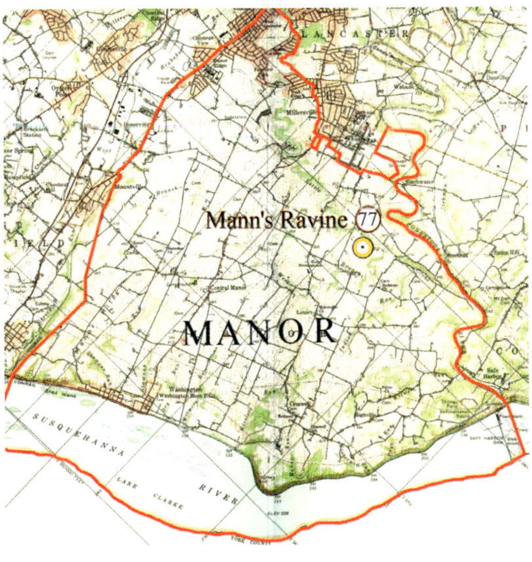

Manor Township. Topo. Kiln No. 77. N39.981053 W76.377393.

Nos. 78, 79, and 80: Hammer Creek Lime Kilns

78

79

80

Left: Hammer Creek Lime Kiln (No. 78)

Top Right: Hammer Creek Lime Kiln (No. 79)

Bottom rRght: Hammer Creek Lime Kiln (No. 80)

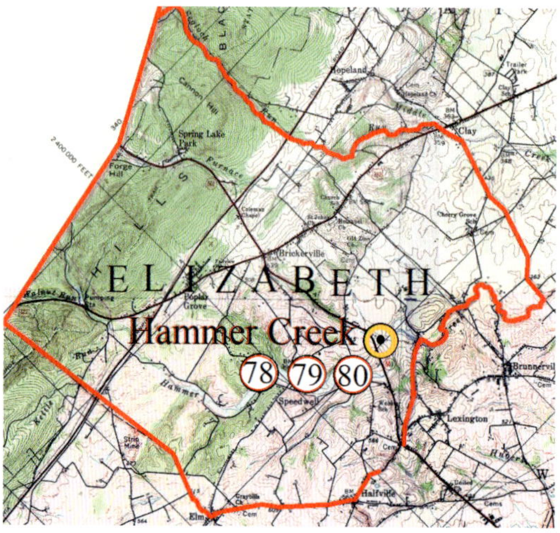

Elizabeth Township. Topo. Kiln Nos. 78, 79, and 80. N40.204250 W76.297413.

About 4 miles north of Lititz, along Route 501, roughly a half mile north of the Hammer Creek Bridge, are three lime kilns hidden in the bank by brush and trees. They are individual kilns, each with its own unique construction and in different stages of decay. No. 78 (*above*), constructed of limestone slabs, is the most complete yet is barely supported by a sagging iron lintel. To its right are the remains of No. 79, constructed with sandstone blocks, with part of the arch and right side remaining. The third kiln (No. 80) has but a part of the left front and an iron lintel showing. A neighbor related to the author how several years ago he accosted a stranger taking down stones and loading them into his pickup, having made no contact with the owner. Possibly they were from No. 79, since the missing sandstones are not found in front of the kiln. None of these kilns are shown on the 1875 atlas, suggesting that they were built after that time.

No. 81: Slackwater Lime Kiln

81

Slackwater Lime Kiln (No. 81)

Close-up of the brick-lined pot

Foundation of the house where some of the lime kiln stones were used

Inside the Slackwater kiln pot, coated with mosses and several ferns

In the center of the photo (*above*), enshrouded in thick brush, one can barely recognize the brickwork of a lime kiln. It is 100 yards from the Slackwater Bridge on a steep hillside above the lane leading to the Shertzer (2015) farm, the same farm where we find the Shertzer Lime Kiln (No. 1).

The limestones facing the kiln were removed—according to Ken Shertzer, the current owner of the farm—by his grandfather, who when moving off the farm removed them to use in building the foundation of his new home along Millersville Pike (Route 741). This is the story as told by the current owner:

> The family once had a dog that roamed the farm, as many farm dogs frequently do. One day they realized that she had not been seen for several days, and they went out on a searching party with several of the family. While covering the farm, calling her name, someone heard a faint bark and, following the sound, came upon the old lime kiln.
>
> There was the doggie, safe and sound, but down in the bottom of the kiln. The old arch at the bottom had long since been closed up. Now these kilns are usually about 12 feet deep, and for some reason there wasn't a ladder available. One of the folks came up with the idea of getting a long plank from a woodpile nearby. They tacked pieces of lath at short intervals and slid the contraption down into the kiln. And Mr. Shertzer said, "She walked right up the plank."

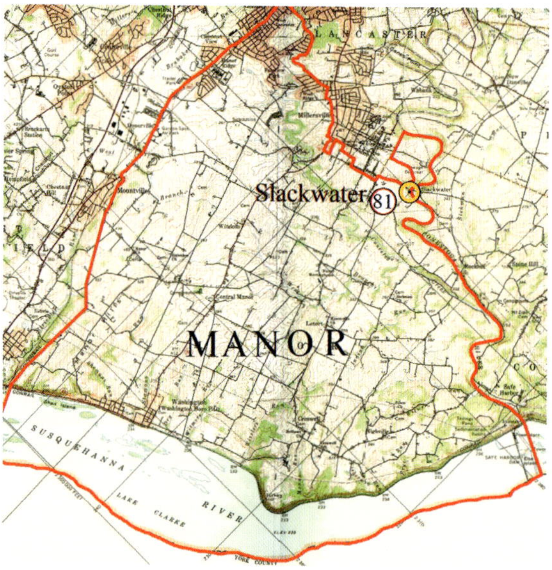

Manor Township. Topo. Kiln No. 81. N39.984328 W76.357670.

It was a surprise to discover this little, relatively uncommon "walking fern" (*Camptosorus rhizophyllus*) growing on the wall of the pot. It gets its name from the fact that the tips of the fronds attach to the ground with tiny roots and develop into a new plant.

"She walked right up the plank."

No. 82: "Lichty's Church" Lime Kiln

82

"Lichty's Church" Lime Kiln (No. 82)

Hidden in the brush along the north side of Union Grove Road, 1.5 miles east of Route 625, these ruins rest on the edge of a small grassy hollow across the road from Lichty's Mennonite Church. A mound of dirt excavated by groundhogs conceals the arch and, if removed, would probably reveal sloping sides. An old quarry bank 100 yards off to the side, which no doubt supplied the stone to be burned in the kiln, forms the opposite side of the hollow.

When searching for kilns, I find that cows are the most curious creatures, as seen with the Holstein peering down at the stranger wandering in her meadow. Some 200 yards east, along the road, a lintel and other stones indicate the bare remains of another kiln (No. 115), more of which could likely be uncovered.

Lichty's Mennonite Church

Caernarvon Township. Topo. Kiln No. 82. N40.149651 W75.999836.

No. 83: Paradise Meadow Lime Kiln

83

Paradise Meadow Lime Kiln (No. 83)

Three-tenths of a mile south of Paradise and Route 30, the remains of this interesting crumbling lime kiln may be found along the fence row in the middle of a patch of farmland.

The use of long, thin limestone slabs in building the massive arch creates an artistic fanlike appearance in this kiln. This design is unique among our Lancaster County lime kilns, and its gradual deterioration is unfortunate.

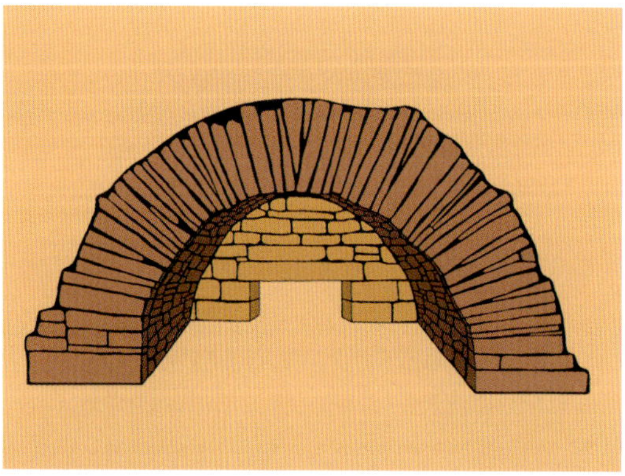

Cartoon of Paradise Meadow Lime Kiln, emphasizing the fanlike arch of thin stone slabs

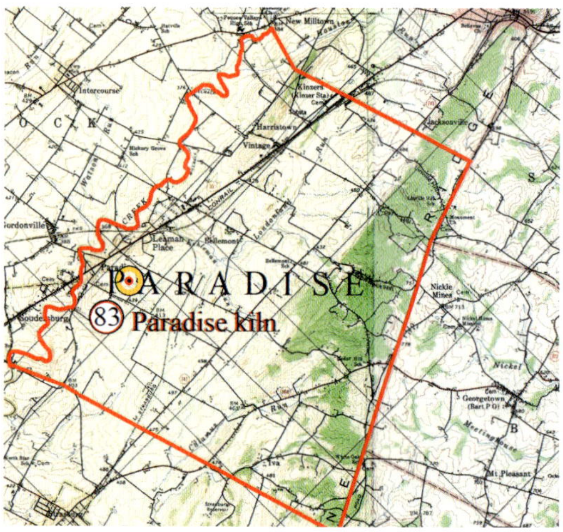

Paradise Township. Topo. Kiln No. 83. N40.062276 W76.221812.

No. 84: Shirk's Meadow Lime Kiln

84

Shirk's Meadow Lime Kiln (No. 84)

A green heron along the Conestoga, near the lime kiln

This crumbling lime kiln may be found in "Shirk's Meadow," across the Conestoga from Ike Shirk's Lime Kiln (No. 35).

Time and the forces of nature have taken their toll, and we don't know its story. The meadow in which it stands and the stream that flows by it have left a legacy that may be found in some old property deeds.

The story begins to unfold with the last will and testament of Philip Bechard, who in 1822 divided his 125-acre plantation equally among his two sons. Several interesting provisions in that will and subsequent deeds that bear on this property, as well as on Ike Shirk's Lime Kiln (No. 35), are presented.

Caernarvon Township. Topo. Kiln No. 84. N40.131476 W75.950832.

Philip Bechard's Will

During the summer of 1822, Caernarvon Township farmer Philip Bechard Sr. composed his last will and testament, in which his 125-acre farm was to be equally divided between his two sons, Philip Jr. and John, as is indicated on the labeled Google Earth image shown. As noted, the Conestoga River meanders through the two tracts from east to west, bordered by low meadows on each of the sons' tracts.

An interesting condition in the senior Bechard's will regarding these meadows that found its way into John Bechard's deed reads as follows:

> the water for watering and refreshing the meadow on the said land shall be used by my son, Philip, the three first days of each week, and by my son John the latter part of each week, the expense of cleansing and repairing and keeping up the dam and races to be equally born by them.

Footbridge at the "fording" to "Shirk's Meadow," near the kiln

The fording would apparently have been somewhere near where the stream crosses the line between the two tracts, with raceways diverting the stream through the respective meadows.

Another interesting condition regarding the use of the stream is found in later deeds. In 1828, Philip Bechard Jr. sold the lower half of his tract to Robert Jenkins, with their boundary line running along the north side of the stream. Deeded to Jenkins were

Plot showing Philip Bechard's indenture of 1822

> twenty eight acres and twenty eight perches of land, subject and liable to free and uninterrupted right, liberty, and privilege of passing and re-passing at all times and seasons, from the line of the above described tract [at the fording] for watering cattle [red dot on map].

The large photo is a view across the Conestoga that is believed to be the location of the "fording," looking south into John Bechard's meadow.

Ike Shirk's Lime Kiln (No. 35) is also referred to in Philip Bechard's will:

> It is also my will that my son Philip have the privilege of burning lime in the kiln now erected on John's part of the land, during his life, he finding fuel being cut, and one half the expense of repairing and keeping up the said kiln, so long as he shall use it.

The lime kiln ruins referred to previously as Shirk's Meadow Lime Kiln (No. 84) are south across the stream, beyond the trees in the picture, but they are not mentioned in either will or deed. Note: Bechard is alternatively referred to in deeds as Bechart, Bechert, and Beckard.

Nos. 85a and 85b: White Oak Road Lime Kilns

White Oak Road Lime Kiln (No. 85a)

The double kilns, showing crumbling Kiln No. 85b on the left.

This deteriorating set of lime kilns rests in the bank on the north side of White Oak Road, just around the corner from Beaver Valley Pike (Route 222) in Strasburg Township.

This is a classic example of the damage that is often done when trees get a foothold in these old kilns. It is furthermore interesting to note that the heavy keystone-shaped blocks that form the main arch are as much cosmetic as functional, as seen especially on the right kiln (No. 85b), where the front blocks have fallen out and the slablike stones that make up the main part of the arch appear to be providing the primary support. They seem to be holding the structure in place surprisingly well. The kiln on the left (No. 85a) is not holding up as well. Both arches are threatened by trees growing up, in, and above them. The following photos show some other kilns that have had to contend with competition from trees.

Strasburg Township. Topo. Kiln Nos. 85a and 85b. N39.926325 W76.194496.

White Oak Road Lime Kiln (No. 85a)

Parke Rohrer's Lime Kiln (No. 68)

Voganville Road Lime Kiln (No. 33)

Millwood Road Lime Kiln (No. 30)

Metzler's Road Lime Kiln (No. 49)

White Horse Lime Kiln (No. 57)

Walnut Hill Road Lime Kiln (No. 114)

Dicely Farm Lime Kiln (No. 66)

Skillfully dry-laid stone walls that are now struggling survivors. Thousands of miles of stone fences running throughout the forests of New England attest to the art and skill of old fence builders. Stones laboriously gathered from fields were carefully matched and fit in between and atop one another, creating fence walls that would last for centuries, although the words of Robert Frost's poem "Mending Wall" will no doubt outlast his fence.

The lime kiln builders, using similar techniques, built rectangular "boxes" dug into a bank, with a truncated egg-shaped chamber inside. Spaces between the stones were sometimes sealed with mud or mortar, and the gap between the walls was filled with red clay, making a very stable structure that could withstand intense heat and physical abuse. Once they were abandoned, there was little cause for them to collapse. Some were dismantled for the stones to be reused in building other walls, foundations, and bridges.

Their cracks and gaps provide favorable sites for seeds of all kinds to germinate, with roots finding their way into the walls. Unhindered, the roots of trees reach down and in time push the walls outward until they eventually collapse. Many of our kilns suffer this kind of damage, with this process being the principal cause for the collapse of most kilns. The pictures illustrate what happens as trees and roots approach maturity and the kiln walls eventually give way.

No. 86: Covered Bridge Road Lime Kiln

86

Covered Bridge Road Lime Kiln (No. 86)

Schematic of the original kiln

Hidden in the woods east of Marticville along Covered Bridge Road, approximately 200 yards south of the covered bridge over Pequea Creek, we find these remains of what appears to have once been a handsome lime kiln, now collapsed and covered with vines, ferns, and moss.

The stones that once formed the left front of the kiln are gone, suggesting they were removed to extend their life in some other wall or foundation. The schematic suggests the original outline.

Martic Township. Topo. Kiln No. 86. N39.929155 W76.297082.

Nos. 87 and 88: Valley View Road Lime Kilns

87

88

Valley View Road Lime Kiln ruins (No. 87)

Valley View Road Lime Kiln ruins (No. 88)

The remains of Kilns No. 87 and No. 88 are hidden in a rocky woodlot 150 yards across the field from Valley View Road and a quarter mile north of Risser's Mill Road in Mount Joy Township.

As seen, the front and arches are nearly hidden in debris and probably could be restored somewhat by excavating the area in front of them. The small quarry that supplied the stone for the kilns is over the rise in the trees behind them.

Location of the lime kilns in the woods across the field from Valley View Road

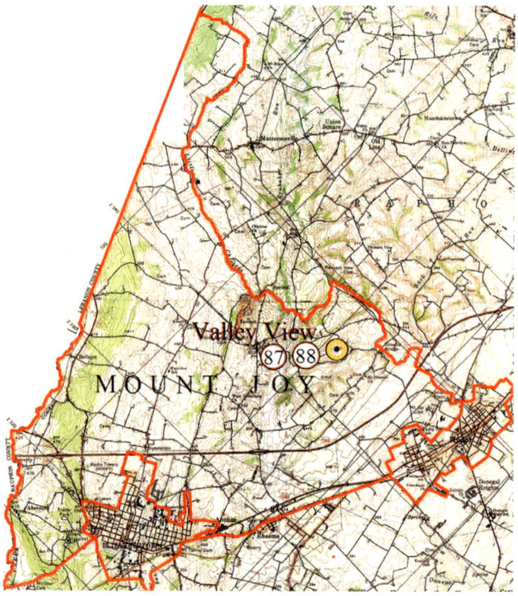

Mount Joy Township. Topo. Kiln No. 87. N40.143070 W76.515963.

No. 89: "Little Silver Mine Lime Kiln"

89

"Little Silver Mine Lime Kiln" (No. 89)

Abutting the Silver Mine Lime Kiln (No. 45) we find this smaller, unrestored kiln, the lower half of which is relatively intact. This little one may have been cleaned up a bit, but we applaud the decision to preserve it in a more natural state reflecting its historical character.

The *Geology Guide to Pequea Silver Mine* pamphlet written by Dr. Wise is sometimes available in a box at the parking lot; it includes a brief discussion of the kilns (it is also available online at www.pequeatwp.org/wp-content/uploads/2014/Pequea-Township-Park). Their specific history, like the vast majority of our old kilns, is unknown. About the most we can do is to search property deeds to see who might have owned the land around the time the kilns were likely built. The few extant kilns that can be dated were built during the later quarter of the nineteenth century.

The "Little Kiln" shown beside the larger Silver Mine Lime Kiln

Pequea Township. Topo. Kiln No. 89. N39.945314 W76.313269.

No. 90: Brenneman Road Lime Kiln

90

Brenneman Road Lime Kiln (No. 90)

View of the ruins from across the field

Close-up of the pot, showing the use of smaller stones in the lining

These ruins are in the meadow just off Brenneman Road, about two-thirds of a mile north of Beaver Valley Pike (Route 222).

When a lime kiln disappears, usually the last thing to go is the rear wall of the pot, or burning chamber. Usually its demise will be slow. Oftentimes the arch will collapse first, and maybe some of the stones will be reused elsewhere. The stones lining the pot usually don't make good building stones, so this part remains, often for many years, until eventually the farmer clears it all away.

As to the remains above, the farmer mused, "Yes, I've often thought about bulldozing it away, but you know, somebody built that kiln!" If that sentiment had prevailed earlier, the kiln might still be standing.

Strasburg Township. Topo. Kiln No. 90. N39.958990 W76.231284.

No. 91: Safe Harbor Park Lime Kiln

Safe Harbor Park Lime Kiln (No. 91)

Schematic of the former kiln

The Conestoga River where it flows by the kiln

This collection of moss-covered rocks, rotting logs, and leaf debris is actually what remains of a lime kiln. It is along Warehouse Road on the west side of the river, 500 yards downstream from the Conestoga River bridge.

It is well hidden by vegetation in the summertime and takes a good eye to find it in the winter. The bright-green stack of rocks in the middle is the right side of the old arch, and the flat lintel can be seen extending to the left. Slightly above and behind them is the hollow remains of the pot. A little tender loving care to clean things up might uncover more of the kiln walls but at the same time destroy the rustic scene.

The community of Safe Harbor, which today is represented by a handful of scattered houses, was once a thriving village. An interesting short article written by Ad Crable for the *Lancaster Newspaper*, September 14, 2004, describes some of the fascinating history of Safe Harbor sites along a walking trail that wanders through the area. It may be found online at https://lancasteronline.com/news/safe-harbor-s-trail-of-history/article_fdfac9b9-caac-5bab-a31e-40a787d456d0.html.

Conestoga Township. Topo. Kiln No. 91. N39.937386 W76.388031.

No. 92: Shenk's Ferry Lime Kiln

92

Shenk's Ferry Lime Kiln (No. 92)

Trillium erectum? White or cream variety.

Trillium erectum? Pink variety.

In Shenk's Ferry Wildflower Preserve, a quarter of a mile from the river on the bank of Green Hill Road, we find this structure.

Yep, it's a lime kiln, or what is left of one! What we see is this large, flat stone lintel, a few rocks still supporting it on the left, and the narrow cavity beneath. Above and behind is a deep hole—the remains of the pot. It is likely that more of the wall still remains behind the soil in front.

The kiln is dug into the bank near the power line on the steep, gravel road leading out of the preserve, in one of the many ravines leading into the Susquehanna River. The road is difficult at best and impassable at times.

The sanctuary is widely known for its large collection of spring wildflowers, especially for a large, lovely population of trillium. There is considerable variation within the population in the petals, shape, and color, as well as among the leaves. Botanists debate its classification, many believing it to be the white variety of the red trillium (*Trillium erectum* var. *album*). One friend refers to it as Shenk's Ferry trillium. Might it be an example of a "hybrid swarm"?

Conestoga Township. Topo. Kiln No. 92. N39.902078 W76.362468.

Nos. 93-100: Billmeyer Quarry Lime Kiln Complex

Billmeyer Quarry Lime Kiln Complex (Nos. 93–100)

Along the railroad tracks and the Conoy Trail, about 1.5 miles south of Bainbridge, we see this set of five to eight kilns. They are just remnants of a once-thriving limestone quarry and lime-burning operation that are visible.

This quarrying operation has a long and involved history, beginning with John Haldeman in 1846 and passing through a series of owners and operators, principal of whom were Haldeman, George Billmeyer, and John E. Baker until the 1950s, when the plant was no longer productive.

"During WWI there were as many as 700 men working at the Billmeyer Plant," where a small village housing as many as five hundred men grew up along the tracks. During its tenure, an impressive array of kilns of many types were employed, including at one time "forty-five upright shaft kilns." The huge quarries are now filled with water and were owned and used until recently by the Bainbridge Scuba Center.

In trying to interpret the existing structures, we believe there would have been stacks above each kiln to a certain height. Somewhere above the current "top" of the kilns would have been doors to receive the broken-down limestone. The double arches above each large arch would be where the kilns were fired. Operators would have worked on a platform extending out toward the viewer, attached where the concrete shows above the main arches.

The burnt lime, or quicklime, would then have been removed from the large arches at ground level. The complete history of this operation, from which some of this information came, was downloaded from an unidentified source on the internet, titled "Words and Works" (www.divebsc.com/Files/BSCHistoryScanned6Nov08.pdf). Another interesting and very informative article by Ad Crable may be found at http://lancasteronline.com.

Billmeyer Quarry and Lime Production buildings. *From the website of the Pennsylvania Geological Survey: Historical Photographs. The date of this photo, taken by George H. Ashley, is unknown; however, Ashley worked for the PGS from 1919 to 1946. In public domain. Collection number 436, negative number 352.*

Conoy Township. Topo. Kiln Nos. 93–100. N40.071519 W76.649542.

"The White Cliffs of Conoy"—Billmeyer lime residue

Billmeyer Quarry Lime Kiln (No. 100), along railroad tracks. *Digitally enhanced*

A dragonfly along the tracks near Billmeyer

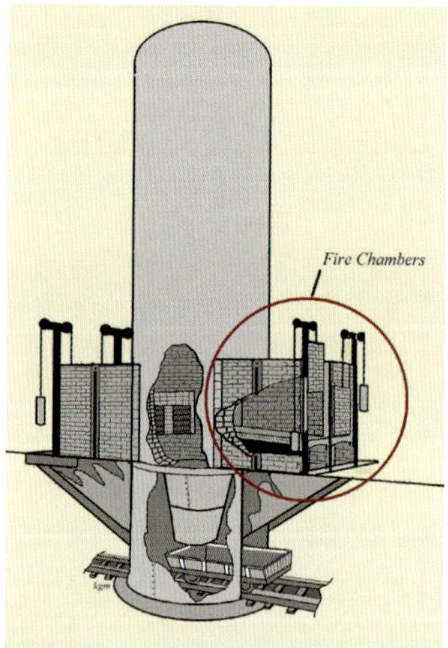

A schematic of a "flame" kiln, showing the fire boxes set off to the side of the main calcining chamber, similar to those in the previous photos

Billmeyer ruins along the tracks

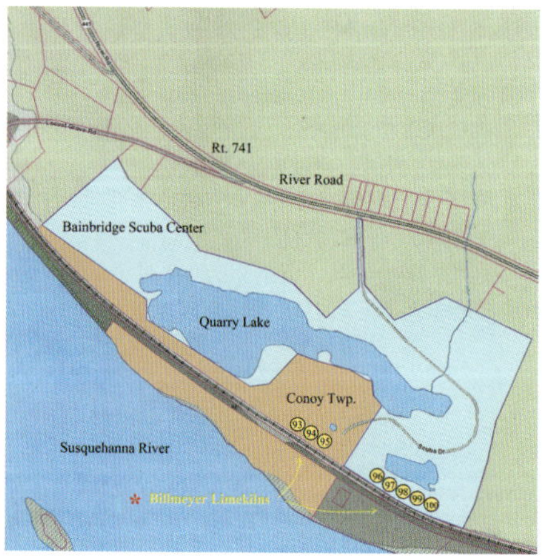

Map showing the location of eight extant kilns along the tracks

No. 101: "Heron Quarry" Lime Kiln

"Heron Quarry" Lime Kiln (No. 101)

On the eastern boarder of Bart Township along Valley Road (Route 2018), approximately a mile east of Route 896, we find these scant remains of the rear wall of a lime kiln pot.

Slag is still visible along the base. Behind and below the kiln is a water-filled quarry. On several occasions when it was visited, there was a group of a half-dozen black-crowned night herons roosting in the trees; hence we named it the "Heron Quarry" Lime Kiln. Its location is depicted in the 1864 atlas, having been built before that time.

Water-filled quarry behind the kiln

One of the black-crowned night herons roosting in the trees around the quarry pond

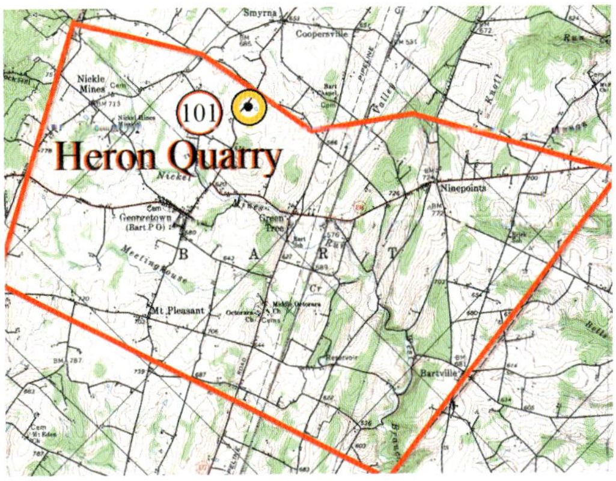

Bart Township. Topo. Kiln No. 101. N39.930676 W76.051197.

Nos. 102 and 103: New Danville School Lime Kilns

102

103

New Danville School Lime Kiln (No. 102)

New Danville School Lime Kiln (No. 103)

These ruins are all that remain of two lime kilns in the woods several hundred yards west of the former New Danville School House. The old schoolhouse, now renovated as an attractive home, is highly visible along Route 741 at the crest of the hill, roughly 0.4 miles north of the New Danville intersection.

The kilns are marked on the 1875 atlas but not on the 1864, suggesting they were built shortly after the Civil War.

Former New Danville schoolhouse

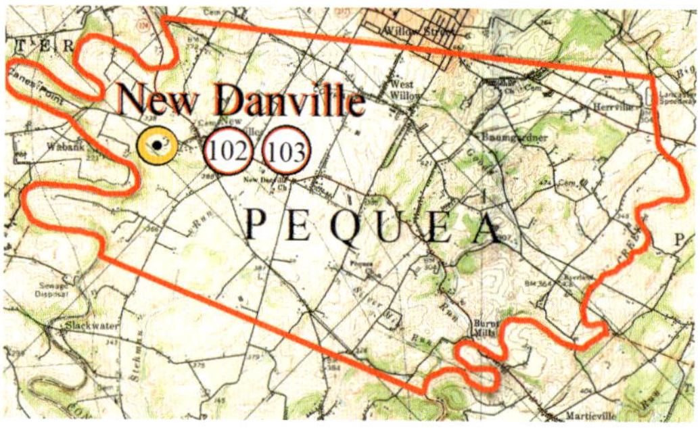

Pequea Township. Topo. Kiln Nos. 102–103. N39.990947 W76.321122.

No. 104: Byerland Church Road Lime Kiln

104

Byerland Church Road Lime Kiln (No. 104)

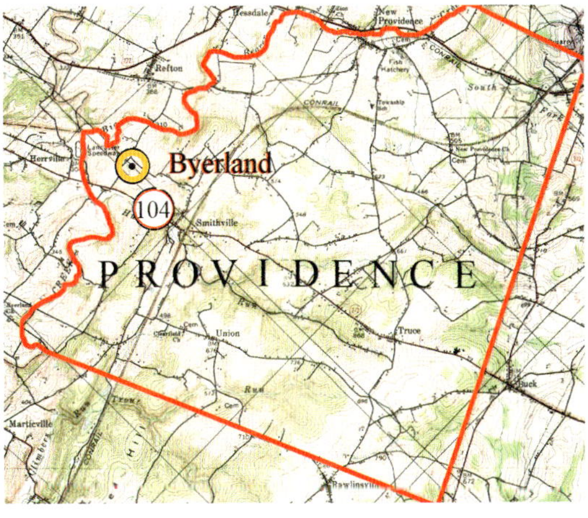

Providence Township. Topo. Kiln No. 104. N39.939309 W76.249975.

Close-up of the heavy stone lintel and archway

This crumbling kiln is at the edge of a wooded hillside overlooking a meadow and small stream south of Byerland Church Road, approximately 0.3 miles east of Route 272 in northern Providence Township. The red sandy soil falling down over the large stone lintel and the front of the kiln is, I believe, fill from between the kiln walls.

No. 105: Drager Road Lime Kiln

105

Drager Road Lime Kiln (No. 105)

Little Chiques Creek flowing past the kiln

Rapho Township. Topo. Kiln No. 105. N40.069310 W76.518337.

Overlooking Little Chiques Creek and Johnson Mill Road, 100 yards north of the intersection with Drager Road and a half mile north of Marietta Pike (Route 23), we find these ruins that few would recognize as a lime kiln.

A few stones still hold up the unusual lintel—a rail from a train or possibly trolley tracks, salvaged when the trolley lines that once connected all the municipalities with their hub at Lancaster City were closed down. Directly behind these stones is the pot depression. On the county atlases of 1864 and 1875 there is a kiln marked at this site, one that was likely rebuilt several times.

Nos. 106, 107, and 108: Mayer Lime Kilns

106

107

108

Mayer Lime Kilns (Nos. 106–109) before restoration

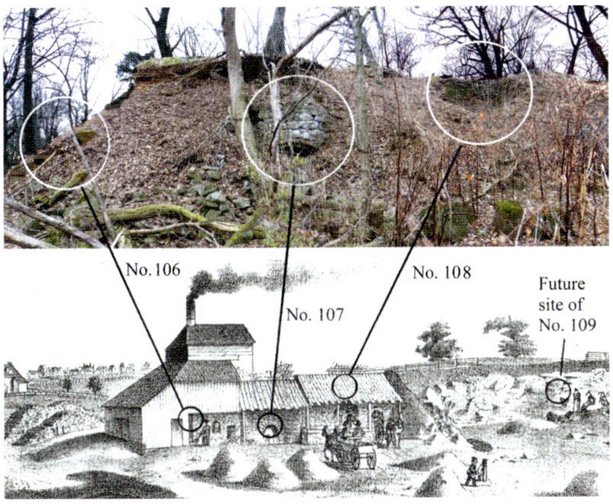

Identifying the ruins through using the 1875 lithograph

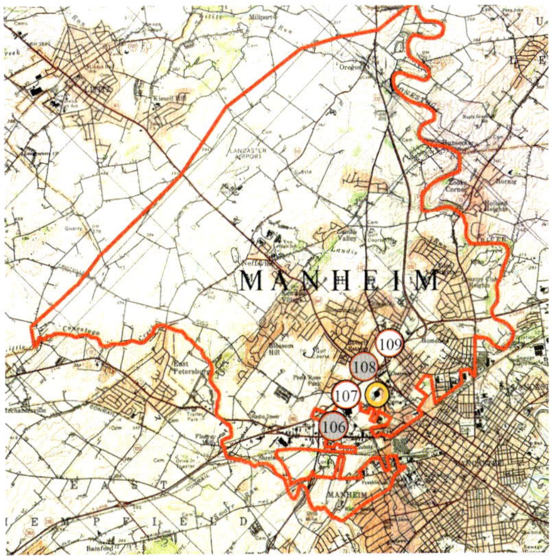

Manheim Township. Topo. Kiln Nos. 106–109. N40.065929 W76.310437.

This lime kiln complex was first built by David M. Mayer in 1867, who around the same time built his large white "Italianate mansionette" at 1580 Fruitville Pike, north of Lancaster.

The photo shows the visible remains of the arch of the central kiln (No. 107) in the middle shed in this lithograph from the 1875 *Combination Atlas Map of Lancaster County, Pennsylvania*. The shed to the left houses a continuously burning patent kiln, the base of which may be seen at the left of the photo. And to the right, the dark depression is the remains of the pot of Kiln No. 109, inside the right-hand shed in the lithograph.

No. 109: Mayer/Belmont Lime Kilns

109

Mayer/Belmont Lime Kilns during excavation in 2017

The site as it appeared in 2018, after the Belmont development and restoration of the kilns

During excavation for the Belmont development in spring 2017, two undisclosed kilns were uncovered a short distance north of the known ruins, thus accounting for five kilns on the site. Kiln No. 109 will be preserved, but the kiln to its right has already been demolished to make way for a road in the development. These kilns are not shown on the 1875 lithograph and would have been part of a later development.

Restored Kiln No. 109

Restored Kiln No. 1. The remains of the pot of Kiln No. 108 are visible (*upper right*).

Turtles photographed in a retention basin in front of the kilns

Nos. 110 and 111: Hartman Station Lime Kilns

110

111

Hartman Station Lime Kilns (Nos. 110–111)

Kiln No. 111, approximately 20 feet to the right of Kiln No. 110

Kiln No. 110 near the waterline (*left center*), with Kiln No. 111 to its right behind the trees

This scenic view of a lime kiln is in East Lampeter Township, near the village of Witmer, in a sparsely wooded copse beside a former quarry now filled with earth and water that has spilled over the area in front of the kilns. The kilns are on the farm of Elmer K. Petersheim, 702 Hartman Station Road (2017). Kiln No. 111 is approximately 20 feet to the right of the view in the photo.

The earth above and around the kilns consists of red clay, which was customarily used to insulate the burning chamber and contain the heat.

Theses kilns are first mentioned in the deed of Amos H. and Clara May Musser, who purchased the 8-acre property at sheriff's sale on March 5, 1935. Since the deed of the previous owner, David K. Hartman, who purchased the land from John K. Hartman on July 26, 1921, does not mention the kilns, we assume that they were built by David K. Hartman sometime between 1921 and 1935.

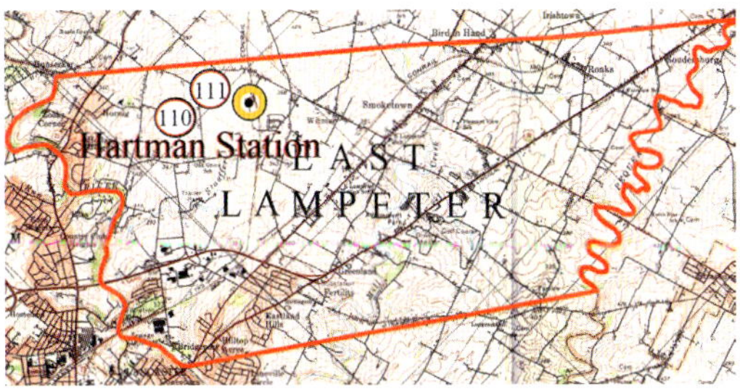

East Lampeter Township. Topo. Kiln Nos. 110–111. N40.062281 W76.221839.

No. 112: "Money Hill" Lime Kiln

112

"Money Hill" Lime Kiln (No. 112)

Coyote paw prints near the kiln

Raccoon prints in the mud nearby

Ebony spleenwort fern growing inside the pot. Note the black wirelike "stalks."

Overlooking the West Branch of Little Conestoga Creek, a tenth of a mile south of Bender Mill Road in Manor Township, and dug into the outcrop known locally as "Money Hill," is where we find these remains of a lime kiln. The kiln is 22 feet long, with the lintel formed by a 7-foot slab of limestone that is cracked near the middle but held in place with a heavy iron bar. Most of the stone front has likely been recycled in some nearby structure.

These old kilns are great sites for small plants to take root among the rocks. Here we seen ebony spleenwort, a common rock fern, clinging to the inside kiln lining. These kilns also make excellent dens for groundhogs, skunks, opossums, and, in some places, coyotes. In the small picture we see that a raccoon and a foraging coyote have left their prints in the mud nearby.

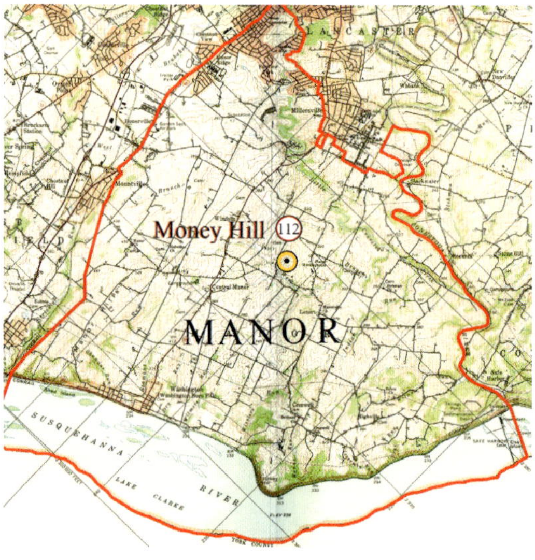

Manor Township. Topo. Kiln No. 112. N39.990147 W76.405193.

No. 113: Herr Ravine Lime Kiln

113

Herr Ravine Lime Kiln (No. 113)

These ruins are visible hidden on a steep, wooded hillside above an eroded ravine cutting downhill, eastward to Little Conestoga Creek, 0.2 miles north of its confluence with the Conestoga River. Visible from a private lane, the arch has collapsed, with portions of the front wall remaining.

Manor Township. Topo. Kiln No. 113.
N39.952935 W76.371470.

No. 114: Walnut Hill Road Lime Kiln

114

Walnut Hill Road Lime Kiln (No. 114)

Along Safe Harbor Road, 100 yards south of the junction with Walnut Hill Road, we see these crumbling ruins of this lime kiln, a perfect example of what happens when several trees take root atop its sturdy walls. The roots in time will find their way downward through the stones, forcing the walls outward with the final collapse of the old kiln.

Manor Township. Topo. Kiln No. 114.
N39.951967 W76.393300.

No. 115: Lichty's Church Lime Kiln Remnants

115

Lichty's Church Lime Kiln remnants (No. 115)

What appears to be no more than a pile of stones on the bank we believe are the remnants of a former lime kiln along West Churchtown Road, 1.75 miles east of the intersection with Route 625. Note the worked stone visible in the middle of the picture, and a slab that is quite possibly the lintel. Other stones are hidden in the debris. There are no records in the 1864 or 1875 atlases of a kiln at this location. A little more excavation may confirm its identity.

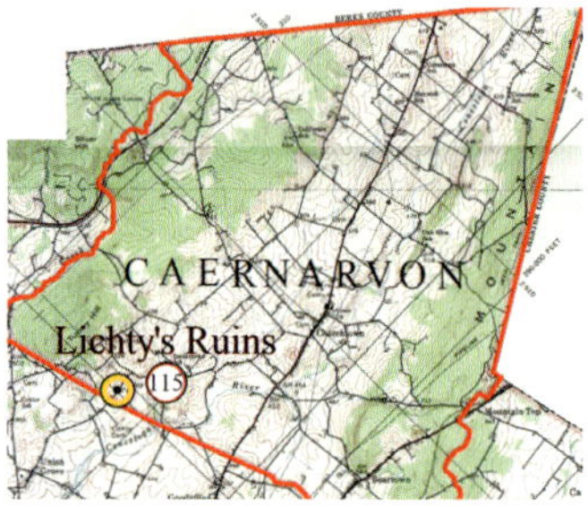

Caernarvon Township. Topo. Kiln No. 115. N40.150025 W75.997240.

No. 116: Pequea Lane Lime Kiln Remains

116

Pequea Lane Lime Kiln remnants (No. 116)

Here we see from a bit of evidence of some stacked stones and an especially old lintel that a lime kiln once stood along the roadside here at West Pequea Lane, 600 yards west of Belmont Road. It is clear that the large, flat stone near the middle of the picture is the lintel, with the archway extending into the bank beneath it. Approximately 6 to 8 feet to the left and right of the opening, we can see the remains of the sidewalls. No records have been found.

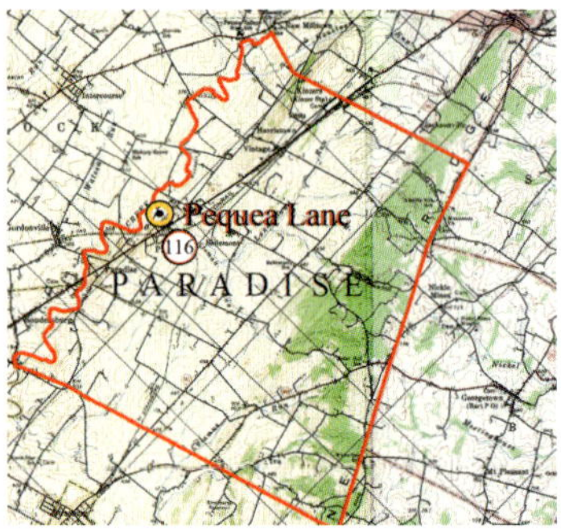

Paradise Township. Topo. Kiln No. 116. N40.016366 W76.116392.

Nos. 117a and 117b: Cider Mill Road Lime Kiln Ruins

117

Cider Mill Road Lime Kiln ruins (No. 117a)

Cider Mill Road Lime Kiln ruins (No. 117b)

Here we see the remains of a lime kiln (No. 117) near the top of a hillside overlooking a meadow along the Conestoga River. A second set of ruins (No. 117a) lies near the top of the hillside, approximately 500 yards across the meadow. It is watched over by a pair of Holstein cows, although the cows were more interested in the photographer than the kilns.

The site is approximately 500 yards downstream from Bitzer's Mill Covered Bridge and the intersection of Cider Mill Road and Cat's Back Road. No records of it are seen in the old atlases. Bitzer's Mill was built in 1864 and recently refurbished with new siding. It is claimed to be the oldest covered bridge still in use in Lancaster County.

Bitzer's Mill Bridge (former Cider Mill Bridge) near the kilns

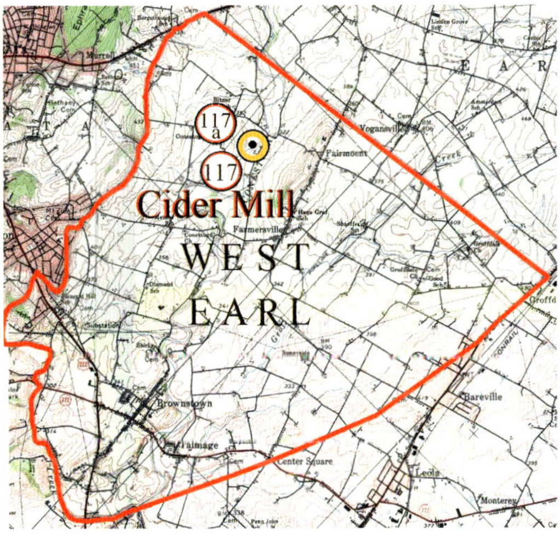

West Earl Township. Topo. Kiln Nos. 117a and 117b. N40.140626 W76.154434.

No. 118: Habecker's Farm Lime Kiln

118

Habecker's Farm Lime Kiln (No. 118)

These ruins are hidden in a small woodlot along Prospect Road, 0.3 miles north of Route 999. The farm has been in the Habecker farm for many years, but the living descendants can offer no insight into the kiln's history; it was just there while they were growing up!

Manor Township. Topo. Kiln No. 118. N40.000443 W76.449576.

No. 119: Ed Hess Farm Lime Kiln

119

Ed Hess Farm Lime Kiln (No. 119)

The remains of this old kiln stand in a roadside bank along Creek Road, 0.3 miles north of East Oregon Road (Route 722). Note the slablike nature of the stones used to build the front of the kiln, contrasting with those of the outcrop into which it was built.

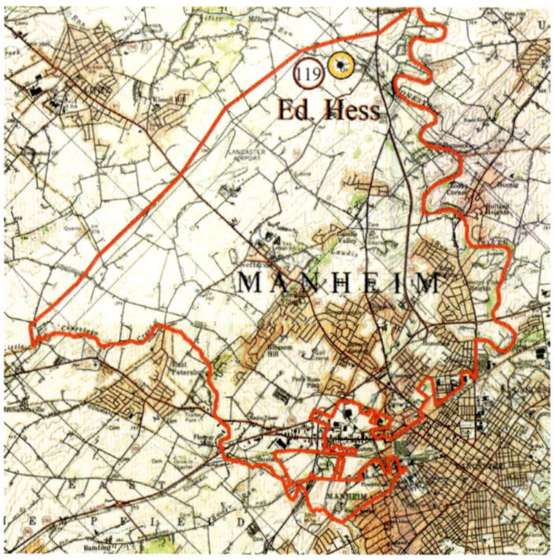

Manheim Township. Topo. Kiln No. 119. N40.117328 W76.251919.

No. 120: Beaver Valley Lime Kiln

120

Beaver Valley Lime Kiln ruins (No. 120)

These ruins are in West Lampeter Township in a small meadow valley slightly west of Beaver Valley Pike, 0.20 miles north of Pequea Creek. The current farmer recalls when the arch was still standing, but like nearly all of these old kilns in the county, the land has passed through several generations or more since the kilns were abandoned, and no one alive can recall their history.

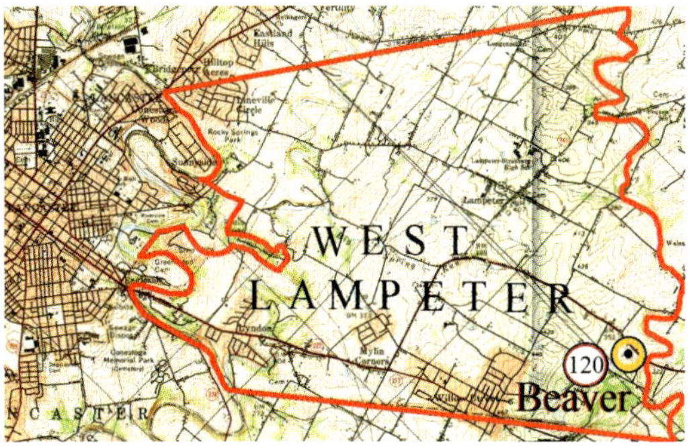

West Lampeter Township. Topo. Kiln No. 120. N39.962190 W76.246758.

No. 121: Wiker Mansion Lime Kiln Ruins

121

Wiker Mansion Lime Kiln ruins (No. 121)

Remnants of the sidewalls and the depression between them mark the location of the pot of this old kiln, hidden on the wooded hillside of a farm lane south of Conestoga that enters from River Corner Road 0.30 miles north of River Road.

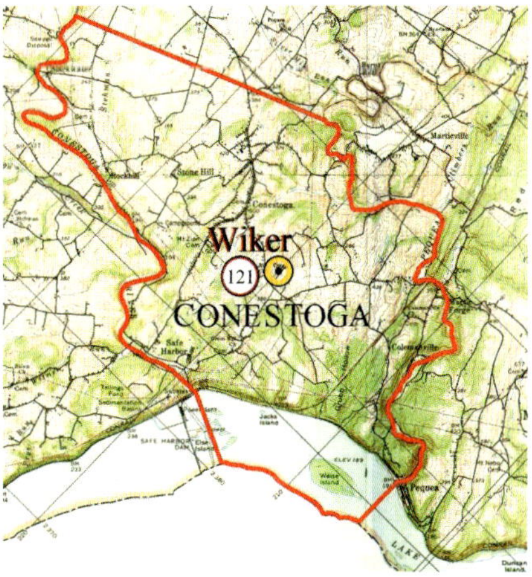

Conestoga Township. Topo. Kiln No. 121. N39.928457 W76.352543.

No. 122: Stu's Lime Kiln

122

Stu's Lime Kiln ruins (No. 122)

This must surely be the minimum amount of evidence to indicate that a lime kiln once stood here. It consists of a small patch of slag-coated stonework with a slight curvature, set in the rear of a clearly discernible cavity in a bank along Pequea Creek Road approximately 1 mile from Sickman's Mill Road. No other remains are visible.

Pequea Township. Topo. Kiln No. 122. N39.921451 W76.321045.

No. 123: Silver Mine Hill Ruins

123

Silver Mine Hill Lime Kiln ruins (No. 123)

The white circle surrounds a barely visible patch of stonework on the bank of Silver Mine Road, about 0.2 miles from Marticville Road; another example of minimal remains of a former lime kiln, one that once stood in the way of modern road improvements. The only clues to a lime kiln are the coatings of slag on the layers of stones.

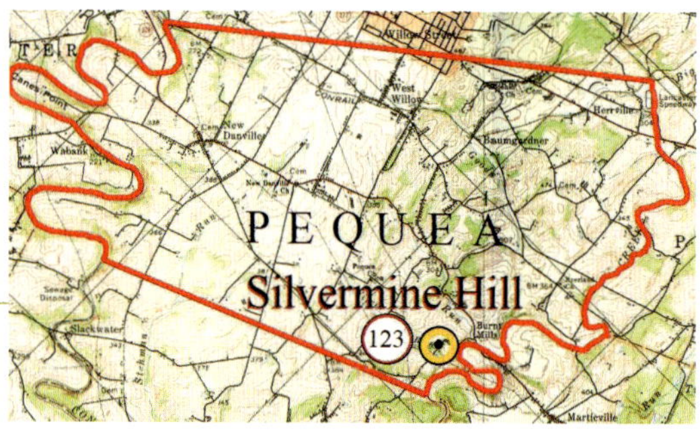

Pequea Township. Topo. Kiln No. 123. N39.942643 W76.308491.

Nos. 124 and 125: Fulling Mill Lime Kiln Ruins

124

125

These walls appear to be all that is left of several lime kilns (possibly three) on a knoll near a large quarry and meadow 0.2 miles north of Route 741, across from the intersection of Wolf Rock Road. Tradition has it that a "fulling mill" once was operated on the small nearby stream. A waterwheel operated a system that pounded wet linen to soften and whiten it.

Fulling Mill Lime Kiln (No. 124)

Fulling Mill Lime Kiln (No. 125)

The knoll showing the location of these two kilns.

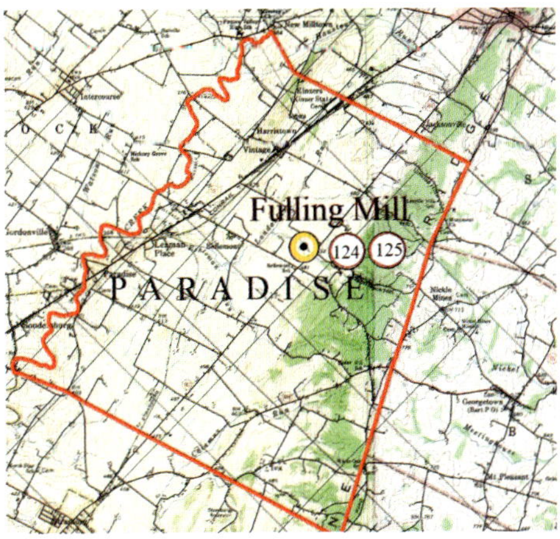

Bottom Right: Paradise Township. Topo. Kiln Nos. 124–125. N39.986631 W76.092289.

No. 126: Jacob Strickler's Lime Kilns

126

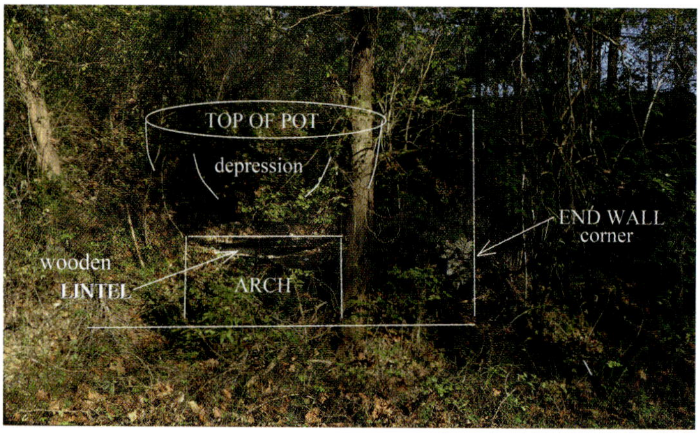

Jacob Strickler's Lime Kilns (No. 126)

Location of Strickler's Quarry and kilns on Google Earth

Hidden in a wooded area 250 yards west of Long Lane and 200 yards north of Donegal Creek Road in East Donegal Township, we find evidence of two kilns once operated—along with the adjacent quarry—in the early 1900s by Jacob Strickler of Mount Joy.

All that remains of one kiln is the lintel and a narrow opening into the archway, with the large depression of the pot above it. Nearly all the stones are gone, except for about half a dozen marking the right corner of the kiln front. The nature of these few stones, and the log lintel marking the arch, suggests that the kiln closely resembled Pequea Creek Road Lime Kiln (No. 48) (*see small image*). A second kiln stood to the left of the photo, as indicated by the "pot" depression and scattered stones and firebricks. Mrs. Velma Andrews, currently a resident of the Masonic Homes in Elizabethtown, remembers her father, Jacob Strickler, working in the quarry and burning the kilns in her youth.

Wooden lintel over the arch on the remains of Strickler's kiln

Pequea Creek Road Lime Kiln (No. 48)

East Donegal Township. Topo. Kiln No. 128. N40.070607 W76.526452.

Appendix

Inventory of Lancaster County Kilns

	Name	Cond.	Co-ordinates	Nearest Road	Twp	Grid
1	Shertzer's Kiln	10	39.980144 - 76.363716	S. Duke St.	Manor	E-7
2	Redbud Kiln	10	39.987961 - 76.369782	Owl Bridge Rd.	Manor	E-7
3	Charles' Kiln	10	40.027694 - 76.376092	Charlestown Rd.	Manor	E-6
4	Prospect Gothic Kiln	6	39.992661 - 76.448031	Prospect Rd.	Manor	D-7
5	Conestoga House Kiln	10	40.049053 - 76.342044	Marieta Ave.	Lancaster	E-6
6	Shenk's Kiln	10	39.997156 - 76.309799	N. Danville Pk.	Lancaster	F-7
7	Brenneman's Kiln	8	39.995851 - 76.309611	N. Danville Pk.	Pequea	F-7
8	Shultz Road Kiln	9	39.990919 - 76.295561	Schultz Rd.	Pequea	F-7
9	Myers Kiln North	10	39.982619 -76.295177	Long Lane	Pequea	F-7
10	Myers Kiln South	7	39.982979 - 76.295001	Long Lane	Pequea	F-7
11	Shallowbrook Farm Kiln	9	39.945708 - 76.242669	Smithville Road	Strasburg	G-8
12	Red Fox Kiln	5	39.983960 - 76.376764	Owl Bridge Road	Manor	E-7
13	Pickle Farm Kiln	6	39.945206 - 76.363286	Creek Drive	Conestoga	E-8
14	Stone Hill Road Kiln	10	39.948273 - 76.345456	Stone Hill Road	Conestoga	E-8
15	Spring Run Kiln	9	39.928944 - 76.370602	Spring Run Rd.	Conestoga	E-8
16	Nissley's Vineyard Kiln	10	40.089507 - 76.646983	Stackstown Road	Conoy	A-5
17	James Logan Kiln (a)	10	39.954398 - 76.369864	River Road	Manor	E-8
18	James Logan Kiln (b)	10	39.954398 - 76.369864	River Road	Manor	E-8
19	Martin Barr Farm	10	39.946895 - 76.217958	Rt. 222 South	Strasburg	G-8
20	People's Hatchery Kiln	8	39.921856 - 76.195822	Main St.	Providence	G-8
21	Camargo Kiln	6	39.920281 - 76.182886	Camargo Rd.	Strasburg	H-8
22	Archery Road Kiln	6	39.903750 - 76.184901	Archery Road	Providence	G-8
23	Penn Grant Road Kiln	10	39.979268 - 76.228334	Penn Grant Rd.	West Lampeter	G-7
24	Rineer's Kiln	8	39.991853 - 76.203027	Strasburg Pike	Strasburg	G-7
25	Gypsy Hill North Kiln	9	40.011715 - 72.270245	Gypsy Hill Rd.	West Lampeter	F-6
26	Gypsy Hill South Kiln	6	40.004834 - 76.266313	Gypsy Hill Rd.	West Lampeter	F-7
27	Young's Lane Kiln	5	39.960960 - 76.358314	Stone Hill Road	Conestoga	E-7
28	North Star Kiln	9	39.996301 - 76.167099	North Star Rd.	Strasburg	H-7
29	Cherry Crest Farm Kiln	6	39.989894 - 76.129570	Cherry Hill Rd.	Paradise	H-7

30	Millwood Road Kiln	10	40.022002 - 76.011366	Millwood Road	Salisbury	J6
31	Snake Lane Kiln	6	40.053343 - 76.030154	Snake Lane	Salisbury	J-6
32	Hartman Patent Kiln	8	40.055618 - 76.226747	Jarvis Road	East Lampeter	G-6
33	Voganville Road Kiln	9	40.096207- 76.124164	Voganville Rd.	Earl	H-5
34	Poole Forge Kilns a & b	10	40.132742 - 75.950042	Rt. 23 East	Caernarvon	J-4
35	Ike Shirk's Kiln	10	40.132865 - 75.949876	Rt. 23 East	Caernarvon	K-4
36	Maxwell's Hill Kilns 1	6	40.144653 - 75.921206	Rt. 23 East	Caernarvon	K-4
37	Maxwell's Hill Kiln 2	6	40.144653 - 75.921206	Rt. 23 East	Caernarvon	K-4
38	Maxwell's Hill Kiln 3	6	40.144653 - 75.921206	Rt. 23 East	Caernarvon	K-4
39	Friendly Ram Kiln	9	40.121505 - 76.254020	Creek Road	Manheim	F-4
40	Amish Farm & House Kiln	9	40.030404 - 76.229522	Rt. 30 East	East Lampeter	G-6
41	Kinderhook Gothic Kiln	9	40.065269 - 76.499218	Kinderhook Rd.	WestHemp-field	C-6
42	Longenecker Rd. Kiln	10	40.103321 - 76.491128	Longenecker Rd.	Rapho	C-5
43	Musser Road Kiln	10	40.101098 - 76.534723	Musser Rd.	East Donegal	C-5
44	Maytown Road Kiln	10	40.093359 - 76.591476	Maytown Rd.	East Donegal	B-5
45	Silver Mine Kiln	10	39.945289 - 76.313101	Silver Mine Road	Pequea	F-8
46	Martin Grove W.	9	40.159016- 76.150548	Pleasant Valley Road	West Earl	H-4
47	Martin Grove E.	9	40.159016- 76.150548	Pleasant Valley Road	West Earl	H-4
48	Pequea Creek Road Kiln	10	39.923217 - 76.326676	Pequea Creek Road	Conestoga	E-8
49	Metzler Road Kiln	10	40.146123 - 76.169499	E. Metzler Road	West Earl Twp.	H-4
50	Lime Rock Road Farm Kiln	10	40.196568- 76.243567	W. Lime Rock Road	Clay	G-3
51	Weaver Farm Kiln	9	40.147476 - 75.990464	N. Churchtown Rd.	Caenarvon	J-4
52	Walnut Run Kiln	10	39.960954 - 76.215623	Bachman Rd.	Strasburg	G-7
53	Deafy's Den Kiln	10	39.919397 - 76.376575	Walnut Hill Road	Manor	E-7
54	Hawkins' Woods	10	39.904966 - 76.355689	River Hill Road	Conestoga	E-8
55	Strickland's Kiln	6	40.103572 - 76.642970	Stone Mill Road	Conoy	A-5
56	Sunrise Kiln	8	39.939862 - 76.391446	River Road	Manor	E-8
57	"White Horse" Farm Kiln	9	40.029618 - 75.994377	White Horse Road	Salisbury	J-6
58	"Bamboo" Kiln	9	40.136068 - 76.117016	N. Railrod Ave.	Earl	H-4
59	Cook's Landing Kiln	10	39.725850 - 76.212266	Cook's Landing Road	Fulton	G-12
60	Mann's Creek Kiln	8	39.994236 - 76.406108	Bender Mill Road	Manor	D-7
61	Gideon's Kiln	9	40.011528 - 75.995816	White Horse Road	Salisbury	J-6
62	Quarryville Kilns (1)	10	39.899988 - 76.143953	Kirkwood Pike	Eden	H-8
63	Quarryville Kilns (2)	10	39.899988 - 76.143953	Kirkwood Pike	Eden	H-8
64	Quarryville Kilns (3)	10	39.899988 - 76.143953	Kirkwood Pike	Eden	H-8
65	Dicely Farm Kilns (1)	8	40.057696 - 76.341781	Harrisburg Ave.	Manheim	E-6
66	Dicely Farm Kilns (2)	9	40.057670 - 76.341802	Harrisburg Ave.	Manheim	E-6
67	Martic Hill Killn	10	39.919402 - 76.307896	Marticville Road, Rt. 324	Martic	F-8
68	Parke Rohrer's Farm Kiln	6	39.948598 - 76.182191	Weaver Road	Strasburg	G-8
69	Royer Road Kiln	5	40.169434 76.221096	Royer Road	Ephrata	G-4
70	Burkholder Kilns 1	10	40.161760 - 76.108046	Fry's Road	Ephrata	H-4
71	Burkholder Kilns 2	10	40.161760 - 76.108046	Fry's Road	Ephrata	H-4
72	Rockhill Kilns a & b	9	39.963355- 76.361542	Stone Hill Road	Conestoga	E-7
73	Ramoth Kilns - demolished	0	40.159206- 76.338368	Limerock Road	Penn	E-4
74	Sheepfold Kiln	5	40.029794 - 76.455381	Prospect Road	West Hemp-field	D-6
75	White Mule Kiln	5	39.940127 - 76.300563	Byerland Church Rd.	Pequea	F-8
76	Lampeter Meadow Kiln	4	39.997679 - 76.247630	Mentzer Road	West Lampeter	G-7
77	Mann's Ravine Kiln	5	39.981053 - 76.377393	Owl Bridge Road	Manor	D-7

78	Hammer Creek Kiln north	8	40.204250 - 76.297413	Furnace Hills Pike	Elizabeth	F-3
79	Hammer Creek Kiln middle	3	40.204250 - 76.297413	Furnace Hills Pike	Elizabeth	F-3
80	Hammer Creek Kiln south	4	40.204250 - 76.297413	Furnace Hills Pike	Elizabeth	F-3
81	Slackwater Kiln	2	39.984328 - 76.357670	Slackwater Road	Manor	E-7
82	Lichty's Church Kiln 1	5	40.149651 - 75999836	N. Churchtown Road	Caernarvon	J-4
83	Paradise Meadow Kiln	4	40.062276 - 76.221812	Oak Hill Drive	Paradise	H-7
84	Shirk's Meadow Kiln	4	40.131476 - 75.950832	Little Hill Road	Caernarvon	K-4
85	White Oak Road Kiln a & b	4	39.926325 - 76.194496	White Oak Road	Strasburg	G-8
86	Covered Bridge Road Kiln	3	39.929155 - 76.297082	Covered Bridge Road	Martic	F-8
87	Valley View Kilns 1	2	40.143070 - 76.515963	Valley View Road	Mount Joy	C-4
88	Valley View Kilns 2	2	40.143070 - 76.515963	Valley View Road	Mount Joy	C-4
89	"Little" Silver Mine Kiln	4	39.945314 - 76.313269	Silver Mine Road	Pequea	F-8
90	Brenneman Road Limekiln	2	39.958990 - 76.231284	Brenneman Road	Strasburg	G-7
91	Safe Harbor Park Limekiln	2	39.937386 - 76.388031	Warehouse Road	Manor	E-8
92	Shenk's Ferry Limekiln	2	39.902078 - 76.362468	Green Hill Road	Conestoga	E-8
93	Billmeyer Kilns 1	7	40.071519 - 76.649542	River Road (Rt. 441)	Conoy	A-5
94	Billmeyer Kilns 2	7	40.071519 - 76.649542	River Road (Rt. 441)	Conoy	A-5
95	Billmeyer Kilns 3	7	40.071519 - 76.649542	River Road (Rt. 441)	Conoy	A-5
96	Billmeyer Kilns 4	6	40.071519 - 76.649542	River Road (Rt. 441)	Conoy	A-6
97	Billmeyer Kilns 5	6	40.071519 - 76.649542	River Road (Rt. 441)	Conoy	A-6
98	Billmeyer Kilns 6	7	40.072553 - 76.651350	River Road (Rt. 441)	Conoy	A-6
99	Billmeyer Kilns 7	7	40.071144 - 76.648765	River Road (Rt. 441)	Conoy	A-6
100	Billmeyer Kilns 8	7	40.071144 - 76.648765	River Road (Rt. 441)	Conoy	A-6
101	Heron Quarry Limekiln	1	39.930676 - 76.051197	Valley Road	Bart	I-8
102	New Danville School Kilns 1	2	39.990947 - 76.321122	Millersville Rd. (Rt. 741)	Pequea	E-7
103	New Danville School Kilns 2	1	39.990947 - 76.321122	Millersville Rd. (Rt. 741)	Pequea	E-7
104	Byerland Church Road Kiln	6	39.939309 - 76.249975	Byerland Church Rd.	Providence	G-8
105	Drager Road	2	40.069310 - 76.518337	Drager Road	Rapho	C-5
106	Mayer/Belmont 1	1	40.065929 - 76.310437	Fruitville Pike	Manheim	F-6
107	Mayer/Belmont 2	8	40.065929 - 76.310437	Fruitville Pike	Manheim	F-5
108	Mayer/Belmont 3	1	40.065929 - 76.310437	Fruitville Pike	Manheim	F-5
109	Mayer/Belmont 4	8	40.066591 - 76.309909	Fruitville Pike	Manheim	F-6
110	Hartman's Station Kilns 1	4	40.062281 - 76.221839	Hartman Station Road	East Lampeter	G-6
111	Hartman's Station Kilns 2	1	40.062281 - 76.221839	Hartman Station Road	East Lampeter	G-6
112	"Money Hill" Limekiln	3	39.990147 - 76.405193	Bender Mill Road	Manor	E-7
113	Mary Herr Ravine	3	39.952935 - 76.371470	Creek Road	Manor	E-7
114	Walnut Hill Road Kiln	2	39.951967 - 76.393300	Safe Harbor Road	Manor	E-8
115	Lichty's Remmants	0.2	40.150025 - 75.997240	W. Churchtown Rd.	Caernarvon	J-4
116	West Pequea Lane Kiln	0.5	40.016366 - 76.116392	West Pequea Lane	Paradise	H-6
117	Cider Mill Kiln 1	0.5	40.140626 - 76.154434	Cider Mill Road	West Earl	H-4
117-a	Cider Mill Kiln 2	0.5	40.142181 - 76.156010	Cider Mill Road	West Earl	H-4
118	Habecker Farm Kiln	1	40.000443 - 76.449576	Prospect Road	Manor	D-7
119	Ed Hess Kiln	0.2	40.117328 - 76.251919	Creek Road	Manheim	F-5
120	Beaver Valley Kiln	2	39.962190 - 76.246758	Beaver Valley Road	W. Lampeter	G-8
121	Wiker Mansion	0.2	39.928457 - 76.352543	River Corner Road	Manor	E-8
122	Stu's Kiln	0.1	39.921451 - 76.321045	Pequea Creek road	Conestoga	F-8
123	Silver Mine Hill Kiln	0.5	39.942643 - 76.308491	Silver Mine Road	Pequea	F-8

124	Fuller's Mill Kilns 1	1	39.986631 - 76.092289	Strasburg Road (741)	Paradise	I-7
125	Fuller's Mill Kilns 2	1	39.986631 - 76.092289	Strasburg Road (741)	Paradise	I-7
126	Jacob Strickler's Kilns	0.5	40.070607 - 76.526452	Donegal Creek Road	East Donegal	C-5

Bibliography

Adams, Terry N. Tappi Connect. www.connect.tappi.org.

Arce, Ignacio. 2003. "Early Islamic Lime Kilns from the Near East: The Cases from Amman Citadel." In *Proceedings of the First International Congress on Construction History: Madrid, 20th–24th January 2003*. Edited by Santiago Huerta, 213–224. Madrid: Instituto Juan de Herrera.

Arthur, William. 1914. *The New Building Estimator*. New York: David Williams.

Bailey, Jordan. 2016. "With Quarry Expansion, Town's Oldest, Most Valuable Industry Endures." *Courier-Gazette* [Rockland, ME], April 21.

Barrat, John, 2015. Corn entered Southwest U.S. first along highland route, DNA shows, *Anthropology, Q & A, Research News, Science and Nature* / 24 February 2015

Blezard, Robert G. 1998. "The History of Calcareous Cements." In *Lea's Chemistry of Cement and Concrete*. 4th ed. Edited by Peter C. Hewlett, 1–23. Amsterdam: Elsevier.

Boateng, Akswaki. 2008. *Rotary Kilns: Transport Phenomena and Transport Processes*. Amsterdam: Elsevier.

Brassley, Paul. 1984. "Northumberland and Durham." In *The Agrarian History of England and Wales, 1640–1750*. Vol. 5, Part I, *1640–1750: Regional Farming Systems*. Edited by Joan Thirsk, 30–59. Cambridge, UK: Cambridge University Press.

Bridgens, H. F. 1864. *Bridgens' Atlas of Lancaster Co., Penna*. Philadelphia: H. F. Bridgens.

Brown, Alexander. 1890. *The Genesis of the United States: A Narrative of the Movement in England, 1606–1616, Which Resulted in the Plantation of North America by Englishmen, Disclosing the Contest between England and Spain for the Possession of the Soil Now Occupied by the United States of America; Set Forth through a Series of Historical Manuscripts Now First Printed, Together with a Residue of Rare and Contemporaneous Tracts Accompanied by Bibliographical Notes and Brief Biographies, Collected, Arranged, and Edited by Alexander Brown*. Vol. I. New York and Boston: Houghton, Mifflin.

Brown, David A. 1998. "Domestic Masonry Architecture in 17th-Century Virginia." *Northeast Historical Archaeology* 27:85–120.

Brunk, Andrew. 2002. "The Claypool Family Joiners of Philadelphia: Their Legacy and the Context of Their Work." In *American Furniture 2002*. Edited by Luke Beckerdite, 147–73. Milwaukee, WI: Chipstone Foundation.

Cameron, M. A. S. 1972. "Appendix IV: The Plasters." In *Myrtos: An Early Bronze Age Settlement in Crete*. By Peter M. Warren, 305–14. British School of Archaeology at Athens Supplementary Vol. 7. London: Thames and Hudson.

Cato the Elder. 1934. *De agricultura*. Rev. ed. Edited by Harrison Boyd Ash. Translated by William Davis Hooper. Loeb Classical Library. Cambridge, MA: Harvard University Press. http://penelope.uchichago.edu/Thayer/E/Roman/Texts/Cato/De_Agricultura/home.html.

Choisy, Auguste. 1904. *L'art de bâtir chez les Égyptiens*. Paris: E. Rouveyre.

Clarke, Joanne. 2012. "Decorating the Neolithic: An Evaluation of the Use of Plaster in the Enhancement of Daily Life in the Middle Pre-pottery Neolithic B of the Southern Levant." *Cambridge Archaeological Journal* 22, no. 2: 177–86.

Conningham, Redmond. 1842. In The Greenbook, Part Second: Narratives and Records to the Present Time. 1888.

Currier, John J. 1896. *"Ould Newbury": Historical and Biographical Sketches*. Boston: Damrell and Upham.

Davis, Asahel. 1854. *History of New Amsterdam; or, New York as It Was, in the Days of the Dutch Governors*. New York: R. T. Young.

Deagan, Kathleen. 2012. *Archaeology at 8SJ34: The Nombre de Dios Mission / La Leche Shrine Site, St. Augustine; Summary Report on the 1934–2011 Excavations*. Florida Museum of Natural History Miscellaneous Reports in Archaeology 62. Gainesville: Florida Museum of Natural History, University of Florida.

Delgougaz, P. 1940. *The Tempol Oval at Khafajah*, Chicago

DePuy, David. 2003. Response to "First Brick House—PA—Letter for Cantrells from PA," posted by Candi DeGrande on April 1, 2003. www.genealogy.com/forum/surnames/topics/cantrell/4294/.

Dixon, George. 1789. *A Voyage round the World, but More Particularly to the North-West Coast of America, Performed in 1785, 1786, 1787 and 1788*. 2nd ed. London: G. Goulding.

Dixon, William Hepworth. 1851. *William Penn: An Historical Biography*. Philadelphia: Blanchard and Lea.

Durand de Dauphine. 1687. *A Frenchman in Virginia: Being the Memoirs of a Huguenot Refugee in 1686*. Translated by "A Virginian." Privately printed.

Eshleman, H. Frank. 1917. *Historic Background and Annals of the Swiss and German Pioneer Settlers of Southeastern Pennsylvania*. Lancaster, PA: n.p.

Evans, Arthur. 1901b. *Minoan Civilization at the Palace of Knossos. Monthly Review.*

Everts & Stewart. 1875. *Combination Atlas Map of Lancaster County, Pennsylvania*. Philadelphia: Everts & Stewart.

FEECO International. *The Rotary Kiln Handbook*. Green Bay, WI: FEECO International.

Finch, Grant E., and George F. Howe. 1930. "The Lime Industry at Rockland, Maine." *Economic Geography* 6, no. 4: 389–97.

Gan, M. S. J. 1997. *Cement and Concrete*. Boca Raton, FL: CRC Press.

Gering, Axel. 2014. "Chapter 2: The Third Working Week and an Antique 'Marble-Workshop-Deposit.'" Ostia Forum Projekt, Humboldt University of Berlin. http://ostiaforumproject.com/?s=The+third+working+week.

Haklay, Gil, and Avi Gopher. 2015. "A New Look at Shelter 131/51 in the Natufian Site of Eynan (Ain Mallaha), Israel." *PLOS ONE* 10, no. 7: e0130121. https//doi.org/10.1371/ journal.pone.0130121.

Hallam, H. E., and Joan Thirsk, eds. 1988. *The Agrarian History of England and Wales*. Vol. 2, *1042–1350*. Cambridge, UK: Cambridge University Press.

Haughton, Brian. 2011. "Gobekli Tepe—the World's First Temple?"Ancient History Encyclopedia. www.ancient.eu/article/234/gobekli-tepe---the-worlds-first-temple/.

Heizer, Robert F. 1940. "Brief Communications: The Botanical Identification of Northwest Coast Tobacco." *American Anthropologist*, n.s. 42, no. 4.1: 704–706.

Hewlett, Peter C., ed. 1998. *Lea's Chemistry of Cement and Concrete*. 4th ed. Amsterdam: Elsevier.

Hirst, K. Krist. 2019. The domestication of maize in America. *ThoughCo*, Nov. 29, 2019, thoughtco.com/maize-domestication-history-of-american-corn-171832.

Historical Archaeology: Original Site of St. Augustine. Florida Museum of Natural History. www.floridamuseum.ufl.edu.

Hitchcock, C. H. 1874. *The Geology of New Hampshire*. The University of Michigan

Hodder, Ian. 2006. *The Leopard's Tale: Revealing the Mysteries of Catalhoyuk*, Thames and Hudson.

Hudson, J. Paul. 1957. *A Pictorial Booklet on Early Jamestown Commodities and Industries*. Jamestown 350th Anniversary Historical Booklet 23. Williamsburg, VA: 350th Anniversary Celebration Corporation. Viewable as eBook 400807.

International Lime Association. 2017. Federation of German Lime Industry, Cologne, Germany. www.internationallime.org.

Jana, Dipayan. 2007. "Evidence from Detailed Examinations of Casing Stones from the Great Pyramid of Kufu, a Natural Limestone from Tura, and a Man-Made (Geopolymeric) Limestone." In *29th International Conference on Cement Microscopy: May 20–24, 2007, Quebec City, Canada*. Edited by International Cement Microscopy Association, 206–265. Montgomery, TX: International Cement Microscopy Association.

Johnson, David. 2009. *Limestone Industries of the Yorkshire Dales*. 2nd ed. Stroud, UK: Amberley. Electronic edition published in 2013 by Amberley.

Jones, Arthur. 1910. *The History of Gruffydd ap Cynan: The Welsh Text*. Manchester, UK: Manchester University Press.

Jones, Hugh. 2018. *The Present State of Virginia*. Frankfurt: Outlook Verlag. Google Books reproduction of the original (London: J. Clarke, 1724).

JUSTIA. 2009. 2009 Rhode Island Code, Title 47—Weights and Measures, Chapter 47-4—Standard Measures, Section 47-4-2, Weights of Bushels, Barrels, and Tons of Specific Commodities.

Kenyon, Kathleen. 1957. *Digging up Jericho: Results of the Jericho Excavations*, 1952–1956, Praeger, NY.

Kingery, W. David, Pamela B. Vandiver, and Martha Prickett. 1988. "The Beginnings of Pyrotechnology, Part II: Production and Use of Lime and Gypsum Plaster in the Pre-pottery Neolithic Near East." *Journal of Field Archaeology* 15, no. 2: 219–44.

Lahovsky, Jiri. 1980. "Cement Industry—Reducing the Energy Requirements in Technological Processes and Heat Consuming Units. Presented at Technical Workshop on Energy Conservation in Silicate Industries for the Least Developed Countries, Pilsen, Czechoslovakia, October 1981.

Lucas, Alfred. 1962. *Ancient Egyptian Materials & Industries*. 4th ed. London: E. Arnold.

Lucas, Alfred, and Richard J. Harris. 2012. *Ancient Egyptian Materials and Industries*. North Chelmsford, MA: Courier.

Lyon, Eugene. 1984. *Santa Elena: A Brief History of the Colony, 1566–1587*. Research Manuscript Series 193. Columbia: Institute of Archeology and Anthropology, University of South Carolina.

MacLachlan, Courtney C., David R. Hoch, and Paul G. Merriam. 2006. *Rockland Area Lime Industries*. Charleston, SC: Arcadia.

Meginness, John F. 1903. *Biographical Annals of Lancaster County*. Chicago: J. H. Beers.

Mellaart, James. 1967. *Catalhoyuk, A Neolithic Town in Anatolia*, London.

Milner, John D. 1972. *The Restoration of the Hans Herr House, Willow Street, Lancaster County, Pennsylvania*. Chadds Ford, PA: John D. Milner.

Moore, Dylan. 2017. "Cement Plants and Kilns in Britain and Ireland." Cement Kilns. www.cementkilns.co.uk.

Morris, Charles, ed. 1900. *Cyclopedia of Practical Information*. The Home Reference Library. Philadelphia: John Winston.

Moss, Roger W. 1998. *Historic Houses of Pennsylvania: A Tour of the Region's Museum Homes*. A Barra Foundation Book. Philadelphia: University of Pennsylvania Press.

National Park Service. 1993. *Castillo de San Marcos: A Guide to Castillo de San Marcos National Monument, Florida*. National Park Handbook 149. Washington, DC: Division of Publications, National Park Service.

Negrón, Tomás Gallareta, Kenneth Seligson, and Rossana May Ciau. 2015. "Ring Structures and Lime Production at the Ancient Maya Site of Kiuic." Digital Archaeological Record. https://core.tdar.org/document/395473/ring-structures-and-lime-production-at-the-ancient-maya-site-of-kiuic.

Netzloff, Mark, ed. 2016. *John Norden's "The Surveyor's Dialogue" (1618)*. London: Routledge.

Paine, Lincoln P. 2018. *Down East: An Illustrated History of Maritime Maine*. Thomaston, ME: Tilbury House.

Pennsylvania General Assembly, House of Representatives. 1841. "No. 28—H.R. 53, Friday, April 4, 1840." In *Appendix to Vol. II of the Journal of the House of Representatives, Session of 1841, Containing the Canal Commissioner's Report and Accompanying Documents*. By Pennsylvania General Assembly, House of Representatives, 474–75. Harrisburg: James S. Wallace.

Penobscot Marine Museum. 2012. "Nineteenth Century Industries: Lime." Penobscot Bay History Online.

Perrot, J. 1960. "Excavations at 'Eynan ('Ein Mallaḥa) Preliminary Report on the 1959 Season." *Israel Exploration Journal* 10, no. 1: 14–22.

Radford, William A. 1913. *Radford's Estimating and Contracting: A Practical Manual*. Chicago: Radford Architectural Co.

Rider, Sidney S. 1904. *The Lands of Rhode Island*

as They Were Known to Caunounicus and Miantunnomu When Roger Williams Came in 1636. Providence, RI: William A. Radford.

Rolando, Victor R. 1992. *200 Years of Soot and Sweat: The History and Archaeology of Vermont's Iron, Charcoal, and Lime Industries*. Burlington, VT: Vermont Archaeological Society.

Rollefson, Gary O. 1983. "Ritual and Ceremony at Neolithic Ain Ghazal (Jordan)." *Paléorient* 9, no. 2: 29–38.

Rowland, Lawrence Sanders, Alexander Moore, George C. Rogers, Stephen R. Wise, and Gerhard Spieler. 1996. *The History of Beaufort County, South Carolina, 1514–1861*. Columbia: University of South Carolina Press.

Sagui, L. 1998 ed., *Ceramica in Italia: VI-VII secolo*. 305–33, 351–82, Florence.

Schmidt, Klaus. 2009. "Göbekli Tepe: Eine Beschreibung der wichtigsten Befunde erstellt nach den Arbeiten der Grabungstreams der Jahre 1995–2007." In *Erst Tempel—Frühe Siedlung: 12000 Jahre Kunst und Kuktur; Ausgrabungen und Forschungen zwischen Donau und Euphrat*. Edited by Klaus Schmidt, 187–223. Oldenburg, Germany: Isensee Verlag.

Schmidt, Klaus. 2010. "Göbekli Tepe— the Stone Age Sanctuaries: New Results of Ongoing Excavations with a Special Focus on Sculptures and High Reliefs." *Documenta Praehistorica* 37:239–56.

Schmidt, Klaus. 2012. "Gobeklitepe: The Oldest Temple in the World." Paper presented at the First Gobeklitepe Symposium, held October 6, 2012, in Sanliurfa, Turkey. Videotaped lecture uploaded by Ozan Guner to YouTube (www.youtube.com/watch?v=J1PDX0NjwsA).

Sears, William, 1994. *Fort Center, An Archaeological Site in the Lake Okeechobee Basin*, University Press of Florida.

Shaw, Joseph B. 1930. *The Ceramic Industries of Pennsylvania*. Pennsylvania State College, Mineral Industries Experimental Station, Bulletin 7. State College: School of Mineral Industries, Pennsylvania State College.

Slack, W. J., ed. 1951. *The Lordship of Oswestry, 1393–1607: A Series of Extents and Rentals Transcribed and Edited with an Introduction by W. J. Slack*. Compiled from John Norden, 1602. Shrewsbury, UK: Wilding & Son.

Sloman, H. J. 1922. *An Investigation of the Properties of Smithing Coals*. Pennsylvania State College, Mining Experiment Station, Bulletin 1. State College: School of Mines, Pennsylvania State College.

Smith, C. Henry. 1909. *The Mennonites of America*. Goshen, IN: C. Henry Smith.

Smith, Lucy Toulmin, ed. 1907. *The Itinerary of John Leland in or about the Years 1535–1543, Parts I to III*. London: Bell.

Smith, Thomas R. 2013. "The Ghost of William Penn: Robert Turner 1685 Letter to WP (Me)—Identified with Public Affairs." *Delaware County* [PA] *Daily Times*, June 28.

Stewart, Henry. 1869. "Construction of Lime Kilns." *Cultivator & Country Gentleman* 34, no. 877 (November 11): 372.

Thirsk, Joan, ed. 1984. *The Agrarian History of England and Wales*. Vol. 5, Part I, *1640–1750: Regional Farming Systems*. Cambridge, UK: Cambridge University Press.

Toffolo, Michael B., Micka Ullman, Valentina Caracuta, Steve Weiner, and Elisabetta Boaretto. 2017. "A 10,400-Year-Old Sunken Lime Kiln from the Early Pre-pottery Neolithic B at the Nesher-Ramla Quarry (el-Khirbe), Israel." *Journal of Archaeological Science: Reports* 14 (August): 353–64.

Torrance, Luke. 2017. "Seven Wonders: William Penn's Estate a Peaceful, Perfect Re-creation of 17th-Century Life." *Bucks County* [PA] *Courier Times*, July 29.

Turner, Robert. 1685. "Letter from Robert Turner to William Penn on the Progress of Philadelphia, 3 August 1685___Excerpts." National Humanities Center.

Valla, François R., Hamudi Khalaily, Nicolas Samuelian, Fanny Bocquentin, Anne Bridault, and Rivka Rabinovich. 2017. "Chapter 34, Eynan (Ain Mallaha)." Cambridge Core, Hebrew University of Jerusalem. www.researchgate.net.

Visscher, Nicolaes. 1650. *Novi Belgi Novaeque Angliae* (map of New Amsterdam with sketch of Manhattan Island). Washington, DC: Library of Congress. www.loc.gov/item/97683561/.

Wallace, William. 1865. "On Ancient Mortars." *Chemical News and Journal of Physical Science* 11:185–86.

Ward, John. 1911. "Construction—Walls, Roofs, Floors, Doors, and Windows, Heating of Rooms, Water-Supply, and Treatment of Internal Walls." In *Romano-British Buildings and Earthworks*. By John Ward, 254–86. London: Methuen.

Warren, Peter M. 1972. *Myrtos: An Early Bronze Age Settlement in Crete*. British School of Archaeology at Athens Supplementary Vol. 7. London: Thames and Hudson.

Watkins, Trevor. 2014. "Klaus Schmidt, 11 December 1953–20 July 2014, Appreciation." *Antiquity: A Review of World Archaeology*.

Wheeler, William Ogden. 1907. *The Ogden Family in America, Elizabethtown Branch and Their English Ancestry: John Ogden, the Pilgrim, and His Descendants, 1640–1906*. Philadelphia: Lippincott.

Worlidge, John. 1675. *Systema Agriculturae: The Mystery of Husbandry Discovered*. London: Tho. Dring.

Yonge, S. H. 1904. *The Site of Old "James Towne," 1607–1698: A Brief Historical and Topographical Sketch of the First American Metropolis*. Richmond, VA: Association for the Preservation of Virginia Antiquities.

Young, Robert & James Garvin. 2002. *A Building History of Northern New England*, APT Bulletin 33. 56. 10.2307/1504796.

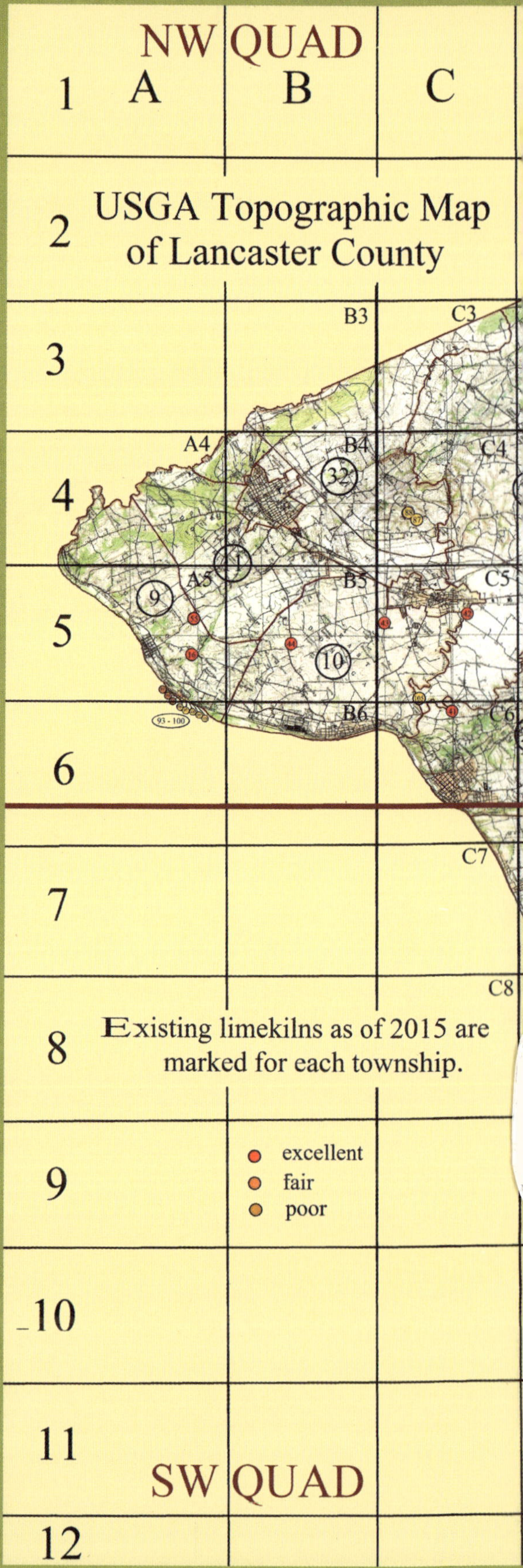
NW QUAD
1 A B C
2 USGA Topographic Map of Lancaster County
3 B3 C3
4 A4 B4 C4
5 A5 B5 C5
6 B6 C6
7 C7
8 C8
Existing limekilns as of 2015 are marked for each township.
9
excellent
fair
poor
10
11
SW QUAD
12